THE LEADERSHIP OF JESUS
TEN FUNDAMENTALS OF LEADERSHIP

"DE OPPRESSO LIBER"

by
MSG Michael M. Cutone
US Army Special Forces

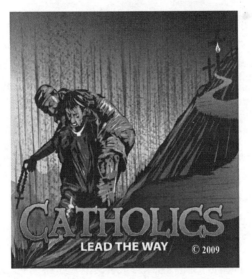

CATHOLICS LEAD THE WAY, LLC.
Monson, Ma 01057

Order *The Leadership of Jesus* at .www.catholicsleadtheway.com

SIC DEVS DILEXIT MVNDVM

Copy Rights / Acknowledgement and Permission

Artwork:

1. .www.catholicprayercards.org. / Public Domain

2. Felix Just, S.J., *http://catholic-resources.org/Art/Dore.htm.*
New Testament woodcuts made by Alsacian artist Gustave Doré (1832-1883) /
Public Domain

Text:

Praise for

THE LEADERSHIP OF JESUS
TEN FUNDAMENTALS OF LEADERSHIP

"A beautiful piece of work. Needless to say, it will be a great help to the priests who read it. But if I had my way, I'd put MSG Cutone in front of every fraternal Catholic officer and NCO organization, and at the podium of every officer and NCO basic and advanced course, and every Newman Center on every campus in the country. I wish that someone had talked to me like this before I stepped in front of my first platoon."

Stan Grip
Marketing Manager / Published Author
Former Lieutenant Colonel
US Army Reserve

"Awesome in its simplicity. I have had the distinct honor of serving with MSG Cutone in the US Army Special Forces and have seen first hand these leadership principles placed into action. Mike is an exceptional leader who has summarized his years of experience into a simple yet profound message. This book is a must read for anyone in a position of responsibility."

MAJ Thomas Sarrouf
Commander A/2/19th SFG(A)
U.S. Army Special Forces (Green Berets)
Iraq - Afghanistan Veteran 2005 / 2009

Soldier's Prayer

"Lord Jesus, I choose to serve you. To fight the good fight,
to shoulder my share; to refuse the easy way out.
Dear Lord, teach me to accept and carry my cross
to the bitter end.

During the hardships and ridicule of this life, grant
me the grace to persevere; the grace to march
towards You with every step, every thought, and
with every breath.
Even though I stumble or fail.... Hope remains.
Hope in You my Lord will always remain.
Victory in Christ. Amen"

WRITTEN BY
MSG MICHAEL CUTONE
WHILE SERVING IN IRAQ 2005
US ARMY SPECIAL FORCES C/1/5TH SFG(A)
ODA 944

SIC DEVS DILEXIT MVNDVM

CONTENTS

Section One: <u>The Leadership of Jesus</u>   **Page**
"Ten Fundamentals of Leadership"

1. Preface   ix

2. The Desire to Know   1

3. The Question of Leadership   3

4. Recognizing the Battle   6

5. The Formation of Priest and The Priesthood   11

6. The Ten Fundamentals of Leadership   13

7. Epilogue   38

Section Two: <u>Catholic Prayers and Writings: To Nourish, Strengthen, and Guide Leaders</u>

1. Catholic Prayers   40

2. St. Ignatius and the Jesuits   48

3. Our Blessed Mother   67

4. What the Catechism of the Catholic Church has to say   77
   about the Eucharist

5. What the Saints have said about Holy Mass   78

6. Why We Should Attend Mass   82

7. The Bread of Life Discourse: Gospel of John   89

SIC DEVS DILEXIT MVNDVM

CONTENTS

8. The Agony of the Garden   92

9. Chaplet of Divine Mercy   93

10. Fifteen Saint Bridget Prayers   96

11. Seven Oblations of the most Adorable Blood of Our Lord Jesus Christ   105

12. St. Anthony of Padua Novena   108

13. What is The Holy Rosary: Origins and what the Saints says about the Rosary   113

14. What the Church Saints Have Said About the Rosary   119

15. The Rosary Prayer   122

16. Work Cited   125

PENITENTIAL RITE
(The Introductory Rites of the Mass.)

"I confess to Almighty God,
and to you, my brothers and sisters,
that I have sinned through my own fault.

In my thoughts and in my words,
in what I have done,
and in what I have failed to do;
and I ask blessed Mary, ever virgin,
all the angels and saints,
and you, my brothers and sisters,
to pray for me to the Lord our God.

May almighty God have mercy on us,
forgive us our sins,
and bring us to everlasting life.
Amen."

SIC DEVS DILEXIT MVNDVM

Preface

The Origin of this book began three years ago as a class, after I returned from Iraq in 2006. A friend of mine asked if I was willing to teach a leadership class to some of his workers. These workers conduct the day-to-day business of his Catholic ministry. I gladly accepted. While drafting the outline of the class, I formulated the 10 principles I've alluded to. *I'm convinced these principles were always present, since my return to Christ; humility provided the moral clarity necessary to distinguish them, and place them into action.* The class was well received. It was later used as a short sermon, and is read by a number of seminary students in Rome. During the following years, I added to the original outline; the result is the book you now hold in your hands. I pray that *The Leadership of Jesus* draws you to a closer intimacy with our merciful savior, Christ Crucified.

What is authentic leadership? The answers you receive to that question will certainly vary, and are largely dependent on the set of beliefs which the responding person holds to be true and important. Why should the definition be so subjective? The answer rests with a simple yet profound failure to identify inherent fundamentals and principles of authentic leadership. When a person fails to understand these principles, he is reduced to applying faulty assumptions; his actions become *reactions*; the reactions, in turn, become a cycle that never quite catches up to events, and the events ultimately overwhelm the man.

There are countless volumes written about leadership, retelling and scrutinizing a specific battle; how a leader rallied his men, rose to the occasion during his darkest hour, then goes on to win a crucial victory; when well-done, these writings are edifying, admirable and worthy of consideration. When well done, they identify objective truths about *authentic* leadership. As a Green Beret of twenty-three years service, I am convinced that we can find those truths in a place where Christians might least expect: the Gospels.

"The Leadership of Jesus," is my perspective of 23 years service in US Army Special Forces, I discuss this conviction by prayerfully focusing on Christ and the Gospels. Christ is the primary example of an authentic leader; and the salvation events of the Gospel are His story. With Jesus, in Jesus, and through Jesus, there is no equal or greater example to teach us the fundamentals of authentic leadership.

The Catholic Church possesses a two thousand year history of unbroken Apostolic succession. The depth of this history is nothing short of incredible; as Catholics we are blessed with the Magisterium, Sacred Tradition, 33 heroic Doctors of the Church, and the writings of the saints.

All of these provide an abundant resource to illuminate the subject of leadership. I approach this topic with sincere humility. By distilling the principles of leadership, the reader is presented with a clear, simple and precise understanding of what authentic leadership is, and how to apply the fundamentals in their everyday lives.

Every action in the physical world adheres to, or is governed by principles. An apple falling from a tree is governed by the principles of gravity. A baseball pitcher throwing a curve ball must adhere to certain principles (Newton's Third Law, Bernoulli's principle, and the Magnus) while throwing that pitch in order to achieve the specific rotation and speed necessary for the desired effect. A marksman firing a rifle at a target has 8 fundamentals of shooting to understand and apply, in order to strike the desired point of impact. If he fails to apply even one, the desired point of impact will be off target. When the baseball pitcher or marksman masters the principles inherent to his specific action, the desired effect will invariably follow. Leadership likewise has inherent fundamentals or principles that govern its outcome.

There are 10 inherent fundamentals of Leadership. Christ, the Gospels, and the saints provide us clear examples. My intent is to clearly, simply, and concisely illuminate *The Leadership of Jesus*. To do so, I will first identify and explain 10 principles of authentic leadership. Second, I will teach how to apply these leadership principles within our daily lives, regardless of vocation or state in life. Third, I will conclude each principle with a reflection, examination of conscience, and prayers.

The second section of this book contains a collection of numerous Catholic prayers, artwork, and writings from the Catechism; also, quotes from the saints and various authors who uphold and defend the doctrinal teaching of the Catholic faith. I enclosed these additional writings to encourage readers in their prayer lives - to nourish, strengthen, and guide them in the battle which all of us face each and every day - the battle that never rests, the battle for human souls.

Many of the prayers in the second section of this book had a significant impact during and after my conversion process. I spent 20 years in an abyss of sin and filth; I admit this not as false piety, but as simple humility.

The prayers in this book are prayers that continue to resonate in my heart, and provide much needed sustenance, faith and hope. I continue to find solace in them each day. Sadly, many Catholics fail to appreciate the immense gifts the sacraments provide…what a sad legacy of poor catechesis!

During my conversion process, through no merit of my own, I was drawn to - and found - frequent refuge in daily Mass, receiving the Eucharist and weekly confession. These beautiful Sacraments provide a tremendous gift of sanctifying graces. Our Lord eagerly welcomes all of us to partake in these magnificent gifts of mercy and sanctifying grace.

During the time of my conversion I found a beautiful sanctuary in the following prayers: I was drawn to **The Fifteen St. Bridget Prayers** which I recited everyday for a full year during

SIC DEVS DILEXIT MVNDVM

2004-2005. The **Holy Rosary**, Saint Francis' of Assisi **Prayer of Peace**, the **Anima Christi** by St. Ignatius Loyola, and the **Memorare** by St. Bernard are my favorite prayers. To this day, I find myself constantly returning to them for strength and nourishment.

　　If Christians only knew the true wonders of the Mass or Confession! Every church around the world, at every Mass, would be filled with souls. Unfortunately, human pride, ego, and sins have corrupted our consciousness. These inflicted *wounds* on human souls and conscious, significantly obstruct our ability or a desire to seek and hear the Truth. Certainly the enemy will do his part to prevent us from ever learning the truth regarding these matters of eternal consequence.

May the Peace and Love of Christ be with you always,

† MSG Michael Cutone

Author notes: Throughout the text the term *men* may and should be easily substituted with the following words: *Spouse, children, co-worker(s), parishioner, anyone under your care.* The word *battle* may be exchanged with struggle or condition you find yourself dealing with; a situation that must be corrected, overcome, or brought to reason. The word mission may be substituted with goal(s) or objective(s) you have to achieve or are expected, required to accomplish. *i.e. be a loving and unselfish parent or spouse, love your neighbor, mentor and lead difficult co-worker(s), live the Gospel each day, foster unity within your family and your work place, be a beacon of light and hope. Lead!*

SIC DEVS DILEXIT MVNDVM

THE DESIRE TO KNOW

"All humans by nature desire to know." This is the opening line of Aristotle's *Metaphysics*. The truth of his statement challenges all men. Unfortunately, many of us choose not to respond, afraid perhaps of what we might discover or fearful we will be compelled to change the conduct of our lives. What is it that all humans desire to know? The truth.

The soul of every human possesses the gift of Natural Law. The desire to know springs forth from our soul. This desire to know is written in the fabric of every human soul; a thirst to know God our Creator, to know the truth and live within the truth. There comes a time or event in every person's life when we find ourselves in the presence of truth. As the morning sun can be painful to our morning eyes, the truth will be painful to the corrupted conscience and soul. Yet within, the paradox of Christianity, this same truth is liberating and healing to the humble soul. A decision will be made, whether man wants to acknowledge objective truth or deny it. This decision, once made, whether conscious or not, will set a course towards authentic freedom and truth - or a course to man's ultimate destruction. Do I acknowledge the truth? A profound yet simple question that carries eternal consequences. The individual is now faced with free will; do I follow and obey truth, or do I reject the consciousness of Natural Law written in the fabric of my soul? Many of us squander this precious gift of conscience from our Lord.

"Man's increasing rejection of objective truth resides in his growing disdain for authority as an intolerable burden. When truth is no longer seen as that which sets man free but rather something from which man needs to be set free, man becomes more at home in the darkness than in the light. This can lead to a paralysis of morality and even to a suppression of the awareness of the guilt."
Paul Kokoski, Homiletic and Pastoral Review. Jan 2008

1

SIC DEVS DILEXIT MVNDVM

"Man is a rational being not because he has a brain, which animals also have, but because he has a soul that is made in the image of God. The brain is merely the physical instrument by which the rational soul thinks as long as the soul is incarnate.

In other words, the brain is needed by the incarnate soul to think, but it is not sufficient, in and of itself, for rational thought. Reason is a faculty of the *soul*, not the brain.

The defacing of the Divine Image through sin does damage to the soul, thus impeding its faculties of intellect and will. The will becomes less free, and more enslaved. The intellect becomes darkened and less able to think clearly. When I had my conversion in 1996 and was looking at a wide variety of religious beliefs, one of the things which sold me on Catholicism was that it's the only belief, religious or scientific, which really explains the world in general, and human behavior in particular. I realize now that what I really always wanted to study was not Physics but Metaphysics."

Ed Hurley, <u>US Army Special Force Soldier</u> (Ret.)
MIT Graduate 1985

This paralysis of human consciousness, grievously wounds our soul and our ability to lead is greatly reduced. All of us are in some form of leadership capacity. Whether as layperson, religious, or parent we have a moral obligation to lead authentically. This applies to every one of us regardless of vocation; *(statesman, military officer, priest, parent, bishop, school teacher, student or carpenter)*. None of us can escape the burden of leadership. We may avoid it, deny it, refuse to partake in it; nonetheless it remains squarely at the forefront, the moral obligation to lead.

2

THE QUESTION OF LEADERSHIP

"Every individual has a place to fill in the world and is important in some respect, whether he chooses to be so or not." **Nathaniel Hawthorne**

Christ is calling each of us to lead in one form or another. Every soul is unique, precious and unrepeatable. From the beginning of eternity God has planned a specific mission for every soul to accomplish. Whether as a parent, teacher, priest, or bricklayer, all of us are called to Christ. Every human is called to love, worship and serve Christ, to inspire and lead others towards Christ Crucified. The struggle for many people is the complete lack of understanding concerning "what is authentic leadership?" Further the lack of understanding that we are all called to lead! This deficiency with comprehension and knowledge regarding the principles of leadership has placed the individual in a precarious situation. Devoid of the knowledge and understanding of these principles and coupled with no training *(regarding leadership)* the outcome has already been decided.

The Catholic Church possesses the fullness of the Truth; therefore, every Catholic who professes his faith in Christ and His Church is ultimately called to be a beacon of light for others, to illuminate the path towards Christ Crucified. Leading others to this goal comes with a cost. The burden and responsibility of this leadership is arduous, and fraught with sacrifices. The lack of good leadership is a significant shortcoming from which humanity continues to suffer.

First we must begin with the basics. What is leadership and why is it so important? A simple question, yet one that so many of us (whether in civil, educational, government, or religious service) fail to answer properly. Why? Society in general confuses management with leadership. Management is a tool of leadership.

3

They are profoundly different; managers do not inspire ordinary people to do the extraordinary.

Christ inspired those around him. He selected twelve uneducated men, mostly fishermen, led the way and set fire to the world with the Gospel message. Leadership is an essential factor in all aspects of human endeavor. Christ is the finest example of an authentic leader; *"As I live, says the Lord, every knee shall bend before me, and every tongue shall give praise to God."* **Romans 14:11**

> "Given the right circumstances, from no more than the dreams, determination, and the liberty to try, ordinary people do extraordinary things. To lead is to create those circumstances, then go before and show the way. "
>
> **Dee Hock**
> *Founder and CEO Emeritus*

Jesus led the way. The Creator of the universe, Son of God assumed a human nature as True Man "The Word became flesh for us in order to save us by reconciling us to God." *Catechism* **# 457**. Then God allows Himself to be crucified by His creatures, stop and think what that really means. The Son of God assumes a human nature, the Word becomes flesh, the birth of Jesus, the unfathomable love and mercy of God enters into the world. During the thirty three years Jesus walked the earth, the three years He preached and taught the Gospel, all of this was leading to His Passion, death on The Cross and His Resurrection, the world is forever changed. Millions of lives, no, countless number of lives have been transformed since that fateful day at Golgotha where salvation history and the beams of The Cross intersected with eternity of the divine plan.

In the past, the church has been blessed with many capable leaders - look no further then the lives of the saints. A clear example in recent time is Pope John Paul II; he heroically led the Catholic Church for 27 years. He played a crucial role in defeating communism, liberating millions in Eastern Europe, inspiring an entire generation of young men and woman, and leading millions back to the Catholic Church. Pope John Paul II truly was an exceptional leader. His leadership inspired many to seek the Truth and follow Christ. The saints provide clear examples of heroic leadership. A beautiful example is Mother Teresa's heroic life caring for the sick and dying. She exemplified leadership in action, living her assigned mission to serve Christ and the poor.

As a whole, the Catholic Church is lacking any meaningful institutional leadership training for its priests and bishops. This lack of the leadership training comes at a heavy cost. Regrettably, this cost is borne by suffering humanity.

"Jeremiah declares that God's way of punishing His people is to give them bad leaders **(Jer. 30:10-11),** while the Lord's way of rewarding them is to give them good leaders **(Jer. 30:21-22).** There is a cost for every fight. Victory is won through battle. **(Revelation 12:7-12)** The truth for leaders? First, victory rarely comes without a fight. There is no success without a fight.

There is no success without sacrifice; there is a cost to every crown. The good news is**,** anything worth achieving is worth the battle. Second, victory rarely comes without a team effort. St. Michael didn't fight alone **(Rev.12:7)**. The saints didn't overcome the enemy alone **(Rev 12:11)**. God designed us to win in community"

John C. Maxwell The Leadership Bible

Providing authentic leadership training for lay Catholics, priests, and religious has a significant role within the Catholic Church. When its members (lay and religious) receive authentic leadership training and apply these fundamentals, the overall

5

effectiveness of the Church mission increases. Developing leadership formation training would significantly benefit the entire church, its members and the mission. Leadership applied is a constant endeavor; it always seeks responsibility and excellence within objective truth.

RECOGNIZING THE BATTLE

"This dramatic situation of "the whole world [which] is in the power of the evil one makes man's life a battle:

> "The whole of man's history has been the story of dour combat with the powers of evil, stretching, so our Lord tells us, from the very dawn of history until the last day. Finding himself in the midst of the battlefield man has to struggle to do what is right, and it is at great cost to himself, and aided by God's grace, that he succeeds in achieving his own inner integrity." # **409**
> <u>**Catechism of the Catholic Church**</u>. Libreria Editrice Vaticana ©1997

The importance of recognizing the current situation with the Catholic Church in America is crucial to having a truthful dialog. An honest and objective assessment is critical with understanding the battle we face and the failure of Catholic leadership.

Our Current Situation: Polling from the 2008 election shows that fifty four percent of Catholics voted for a pro-abortion candidate, prominent Catholic politicians publicly support, promote and vote for abortion legislation. Forty eight million babies have been aborted in America alone since the US Supreme Court ruling on *Roe vs Wade*. Consider what that number really represents. Forty eight million infants. A mother's womb is no longer safe for the most innocent of souls.

6

SIC DEVS DILEXIT MVNDVM

During the horrors of World War II General Dwight D. Eisenhower sent the following telegram to US Chief of Staff Marshall, on 19 April 1945 describing what he has seen first hand:

> "We continue uncover German concentration camps for political prisoners in which conditions of undesirable honors prevail. I have visited one of these myself and I assure you what ever has been printed on them to date has been an understatement. If you would see any advantage in asking about a dozen leaders of congress and a dozen prominent editors to make a short visit to theater in a couple of C-64s, I will arrange to have them conducted to one of these places where the evidence of bestiality and cruelty is so over powering as to leave no doubt in their minds about the normal practices of the Germans in these camps."

The Dwight D. Eisenhower Presidential Library and Museum Website

General Eisenhower understood that Americans back home must have the complete truth regarding the facts of Nazi atrocities "[the] *cruelty is so over powering as to leave no doubt in their minds.* Imagine today if 12 congressional leaders and newspaper editors were to visit an abortion clinic and witness first hand what occurs to the infants during an abortion. Americans would be aghast if the images of these discarded infant bodies were on the front page of every newspaper across the country.

The Nazi death camps were evil, brutal and an effective killing machine; millions of innocent lives were murdered. Abortion clinics in America have far exceeded the most efficient Nazi death camp by ten fold. Our society continues to ignore and properly address this horrific issue; the truth has been replaced with a creative American slogan "pro-choice". The rule of law upholds the

7

destruction of these poor infants. Innocent, defenseless, precious and unrepeatable a child in a mother's womb is no longer safe. How can that be?

Historians have recalled the horrors the Nazis inflicted on humanity and other brutal regimes throughout history. The Aztecs were very effective at human sacrifices, carving out the human heart from a living human being. Any reasonable person clear understands the evil in such an act, yet somehow the deliberate killing of an infant in the womb of a mother is a "choice." Gen. Eisenhower's telegram still rings true today *"where the evidence of bestiality and cruelty is so over powering as to leave no doubt in their minds about the normal practices of the Germans in these camps."* One day history will judge the United States and the same will be said about our abortion clinics. God help us.

Catholic Universities such as Notre Dame honor an American pro-abortion politician with an honoree degree; Georgetown University covered a cross and several monogram letters IHS that represent Jesus at the request of a US politician speaking at the university. The early Jesuits without hesitation would have defended Christ and His message. What happen to our Catholic leadership? Where is the courage, the desire, and the passion to stand up and valiantly defend Christ? When and how did Catholics become mice? Would St. Ignatius the founder of the Jesuits allow Christian symbols of Jesus or a cross to be covered at the request of a politician? Of course not! There are many examples, what happened at Georgetown University is simple cowardness; Christ was sold for thirty pieces of silver yet again. Defending the truth and standing with Christ comes with a cross. Unfortunately many are not willing to endure the weight of their cross. Jesus reminds us, *"Whoever is ashamed of me and of my words in this faithless and sinful generation, the Son of Man will be ashamed of when he comes in his Father's glory with the holy angels."* **Mark 8:38**

The ubiquitous attacks by American pop culture on the Catholic Church and Christianity in general is a daily event. Our universities, the media and Hollywood have done a masterful job at ridiculing every Christian virtue and elevating every form of sin as a noble fight, cloaked under the guise of *"rights or freedom of choice."* At what point and what manner of horror will awake Catholics from their slumber of moral relativism.

All of this is a direct result of poor leadership, specifically with Catholics. We *(Catholics)* have been poorly educated in our faith for the last 30 plus years. Objective truth has become a casualty in this battle for souls. The lack of courageous and authentic Catholic leadership comes with a heavy price. All of humanity suffers. **All of us own a portion of this guilt.** From bishops failing to lead, teach and hold their flock accountable, to priests and religious being negligent with upholding and defending the Magisterium of the Church, to the vast majority of lay Catholics that never attend Mass, or go to confession. Regrettably the outcome is predictable many American Catholics are slothful or not concerned with learning their faith or even attempting to live the Gospel. Perhaps our greatest collective failure as lay Catholics is the lack of earnest desire, to truly learn our faith and pray for the men who are called to lead us, our bishops and priests.

How many parishioners are lost because they were poorly led? This question takes us back to the dramatic distinction between management and leadership. A manager is concerned with numbers, budgets, overhead, and "political correctness." Leaders inspire ordinary men to do the seemingly impossible. A leader is selfless in his service towards others, and towards the mission. The individuals placed under his charge and the mission with which he is entrusted, are co-equals.

Thus, genuine leaders sacrifice themselves to save their men, and to ensure the successful accomplishment of the assigned mission. When individuals without proper training or guidance are placed in a leadership position, the team suffers. In a parish setting, the Church suffers. Ultimately, humanity suffers.

Oftentimes, bishops, priests and lay leaders, lacking any formal leadership training, are frequently overwhelmed when placed in leadership positions. John Keegan, a brilliant British military historian, coined the phrase *"the loneliness of command'*. This phrase truly captures the essence of what a leader will have to endure!

Couple this circumstance with inadequate priestly and episcopal leadership: the results are often predetermined - the mission fails. Scripture tells us that there are certain charisms given to men by God. For some, the charisms are to preach, to teach or heal; and for others, it's the gift to lead. There are ten fundamental principles of leadership. Our priests and religious must be equipped with the knowledge of these principles, and how to apply them.

Authentic leadership in one form or another falls squarely on the shoulders of every Christian; whether a bishop, priest, religious or lay Catholic. Ignoring this simple truth comes with a heavy cost; all of humanity suffers. Growing the capacity of authentic leadership within the Catholic Church will increase the effectiveness of the church's mission; to save souls.

THE FORMATION OF PRIESTS
Leaders inspire ordinary people to do the extraordinary

The Post –Synodal Apostolic Exhortation of John Paul II **Pastores Dabo Vobis** discusses the formation of priests. He identifies four main areas of priestly formation:

1. Human
2. Intellectual
3. Spiritual
4. Pastoral

Each is an integral element within the formation of priests. Pope John Paul II emphasizes how truly important the human formation is for priests by citing the following: *"The whole work of priestly formation would be deprived of its necessary foundation if it lacked a suitable human formation." PDV# 43*

"This statement by the synod fathers expresses not only a fact which reason brings to our consideration every day and which experience confirms, but a requirement which has a deeper and specific motivation in the very nature of the priest and ministry. The priest, who is called to be a *"living image"* of Jesus Christ, head and shepherd of the church, should seek to reflect in himself, as far as possible, the human perfection which shines forth in the incarnate Son of God and which is reflected with particular liveliness in his attitudes toward others as we see narrated in the Gospels" PDV# 43.

This essay will focus on the "human formation," specifically with the aspect of leadership. The statement by synod fathers is clear: *"priestly formation would be deprived of its necessary foundation if it lacked a suitable human formation."* The terms *"head and Shepherd of the Church"* are clear assertions to lead. What level of authentic leadership training (if any) have seminary students received during their human formation?

11

This statement is not meant to be critical, rather a sincere inquiry. These future priests will be asked to lead others in spiritual battle! Make no mistake about what awaits them once they graduate the seminary: **A raging battle, a battle that never rests.**

Preparing them for anything less is a disservice to them, to the Church, and to the very souls who will cry out for authentic leadership. The framework for human formation is leadership. Without this framework, human formation cannot stand and function. The component of leadership within human formation can be developed and nurtured with specific training. Understanding and applying the 10 fundamentals of leadership in daily life is crucial with exercising the development of human formation. Currently, seminary students receive little to no training on the fundamentals of leadership. How is this possible? How can they be expected to lead others?

Seminary students during formation training need to be prepared for the battle that awaits them. Priests are servants of Christ, and ministers of the Holy Sacraments. They are also called to lead! They have been selected from men to be priests.

They are called to lead poor suffering souls to Christ, to be leaders in mercy, in prayer, in charity, in sacrifice, in teaching and defending the Catholic Faith. The essence of leadership is sacrifice, freely giving of oneself to your flock and the mission. Christ provides us with the clearest example. Leadership comes with a cost. Individuals not willing to suffer for Christ cannot and will not lead authentically.

THE PRIESTHOOD
St. John Chrysostom, Doctor of the Church. From his treatise
On the Priesthood.

"The greatness and dignity of the priesthood rise above all that is earthly and human. For the priestly office is indeed discharged on earth, but it ranks amongst heavenly ordinances; and very naturally so, for neither man nor angel, nor archangel, nor any other created power, but the Paraclete Himself, instituted this vocation and persuaded men, while still abiding in the flesh, to represent the ministry of angels. Wherefore, the consecrated priest ought to be as pure as if he were standing in the heavens themselves in the midst of those powers... For when thou seest the Lord sacrificed and laid upon the altar, and the priest standing and praying over the Victim, and all the worshippers empurpled with that Precious Blood, canst thou think thou art still amongst men and standing on the earth...Oh, what a marvel! What love of God to man!"

Fr. Christopher Rengers, O.F.M. The 33 Doctors of the Church.

THE FUNDAMENTALS OF LEADERSHIP
MSG. Michael M. Cutone

There are ten fundamentals of leadership. One must understand these fundamentals; have the ability and willingness to apply them. Submitting ourselves to Christ provides the necessary graces to apply these principles in an authentic manner. Christ Crucified is the greatest example of an authentic leader. He is perfection in every manner. He took several poor, uneducated fishermen and changed the world. His actions, words, and humility continue to inspire and lead others to Himself, and to the calling of priestly and religious life.

The following principles were derived by primarily focusing on Jesus, the Gospel, prayer, teachings of the saints, church history and twenty three years of experience within the US Army Special Forces. A good amount of credit belongs to exceptional Non-Commissioned Officers and Officers who faithfully led and mentored me during my years within the Army Special Forces.

In the final analysis, all the merit belongs to Christ, without His mercy, His forgiveness, and grace I would not have been capable of writing this small simple book. I did not truly understand, nor did I have the moral clarity to understand or apply the ten principles of leadership until I willfully submitted myself to Christ. Only then did the truth and lucidity of leadership become meaningful. Humility is ever so gentle and distinct in the way she opens hardened souls and minds of men to receive and accept the sweet splendor of Truth.

LEADERSHIP

L= LEAD BY EXAMPLE. These three simple words are what good leaders epitomize. They lead from the front. They set truthful standards of excellence, which they uphold and live daily. Their example inspires others around them to follow. The vast majority of people fail to understand and apply this simple yet powerful principle. Still others are crushed by the weight of this expectation on them. To lead by example leaders must have strong moral character and place a premium on virtues. *"I will instruct you and show you the way you should walk, give you counsel and watch over you."* **Psalms 32:8.** God will provide us the necessary strength and grace when we submit our self to Him and to His commandments. Remember, as leaders we work for our mislabeled subordinates.

14

> *"But it shall not be so among you. Rather, whoever wishes to be great among you shall be your servant; whoever wishes to be first among you shall be your slave. Just so, the Son of Man did not come to be served but to serve and to give his life as a ransom for many."* **Matthew 20:26-28.**

We worship and love Christ - in doing so we provide a genuine example for others to follow. Authentic leaders live the Gospel.

Authentic leaders do not ask those around them to perform a task nor give their subordinates a mission that they themselves would not accomplish. Look to Christ. He led by example. He never asked His Apostles to do something He was not willing to do Himself. Christ's words and actions are clear. He provided clear standards for all of us to follow. Good leaders show the way. They lead from the front! They provide examples on how to accomplish the impossible. They lead by example in word and deed. When leaders live this creed their every action and every thought, becomes a witness of inspiration for others to follow. With all your actions and thoughts stay focused on Christ Crucified, His excellence and grace will guide you.

> *"Finally, brothers, whatever is true, whatever is honorable, whatever is just, whatever is pure, whatever is lovely, whatever is gracious, if there is any excellence and if there is anything worthy of praise, think about these things. Keep on doing what you have learned and received and heard and seen in me. Then the God of peace will be with you."* **Philippians 4:8-9**

15

SIC DEVS DILEXIT MVNDVM

Your inaction or action will speak more about you than your words
ever will. Every day, every moment, every thought, and every action
is an opportunity to lead by example…to be a beacon of truth, hope,
and an inspiration to others; to simply glorify God. Christ led the
way with His Cross. To become effective leaders we must embrace
our assigned cross and follow Christ. In doing so we lead others
towards Christ Crucified. The greatest leadership example is Christ
carrying His Cross to Calvary.

*Reflections and examination of your conscience: Do you lead by
example with others or do you cut corners? Do you ask or demand
of others what you yourself are unwilling to accomplish? Do you
choose the "easy wrong" over the "hard right?"*

*Pray: Dear Jesus teach me to live and lead by your authentic
example. Make me an instrument of Your leadership, with every
struggle in my life, may Your wisdom reveal the truth within it;
Grant me the grace to approach these challenges as opportunities
to glorify You my Lord; to provide clear examples of leadership and
truth; to simply and faithfully glorify God's will. Amen.*

Pray the Our Father, Hail Mary, Glory be to the Father

E= EDUCATION. Expand your knowledge, seek the truth.
Educate and expand the knowledge of your subordinates, be willing
to seek and learn the truth in your specific field. Always seek the
truth. Do not become stagnant when learning and living your
Catholic faith. When you truly seek the knowledge and science of
the saints your soul and mind become fertile to the reception of
truth. Leaders must have a desire to seek the truth within their
specific field, whether in medicine, law, mathematics, philosophy,
natural sciences, or a simple carpenter. Perhaps the most important
field is a parent.

16

The future of their child rests in their hands. Leaders desire those around them to grow in the knowledge and science of the saints. The four Gospels provide clear examples of Christ educating and preparing His Apostles for the mission they would have to accomplish. For three years Jesus lived alongside His Apostles teaching and educating them. This is our finest example.

The life of St. Paul provides us an incredible example of teaching the Gospel to all that would hear. He did not sit back on his heels but preached and taught the Gospel throughout the Mediterranean world. St. Paul's journeys also established several churches along the way. Pull out a map and actually plot the locations St. Paul traveled, the different countries and cities he taught and spread the Gospel. A remarkable feat! From Greece, Myra (Turkey), Perge, Sidon, Tyre, Ephesus, Corinth, Philippi, and Rome, St. Paul was on a mission. Our lives are a constant opportunity to seek and to learn the truth, to teach and share the wisdom and authentic teaching of Christ and His Church. Leaders must share this love and knowledge of Christ. Words from St. Paul " *Pray…that speech may be given me to open my mouth, to make known with boldness the mystery of the gospel for which I am an ambassador in chains, so that I may have the courage to speak as I must.*" **Ephesians 6:19-20**

Reflections and examination of your conscience: *Do you seek with earnest desire to grow in the knowledge of the truth? Do you educate your subordinates and challenge them to grow in knowledge of truth? Are you seeking knowledge of the Truth who is Christ which is taught by His Church…or personal opinion?*

Pray: *Dear Jesus teach me to have a true desire to learn and acknowledge objective truth. May I be open to the grace of knowledge, who I am…a sinner, who God is… the Creator of the Universe, and to grow perfect in the science of the saints. To have*

SIC DEVS DILEXIT MVNDVM

an authentic desire to learn the wisdom and truth of the Catholic Church; to simply and faithfully glorify God's will. Amen.

Pray the Our Father, Hail Mary, Glory be to the Father

A= ATTITUDE. Is the passion we bring to the fight. It sets the tone and tempo of your convictions. When your attitude and effort is authentic and robust you will inspire others to follow. No one will follow a "leader" into battle that complains, moans, or settles for mediocrity. A dynamic attitude motivates others and strengthens them with the task at hand. It inspires others to work toward the assigned mission. A positive attitude lifts the hearts and spirits of others. Leaders remain positive and steadfast in the worst conditions, and relish the opportunity to face the hardship at hand. You are in control of your attitude.

The challenge is to remain unwavering in the face of hardship, to provide hope where there is despair, light where there is darkness, and courage where there is weakness. Christ remained steadfast during the Passion: He continued on with His mission. During the Passion, our Lord's attitude and courage remained constant and resolute. His love for man was exemplified on the Cross. Attitude is the passion we bring to the fight, the willingness to fight for Christ. *"For you did not receive a spirit of slavery to fall back into fear, but you received a spirit of adoption, through which we cry "Abba, Father!"* **Romans 8:15**

ATTITUDE

"The longer I live, the more I realize the impact of attitude on life. Attitude, to me is more important than facts. It's more important than the past, than education, than money, than circumstances, than failures, than success, than what other people think, or say or do. It is more important than appearance, giftedness, or skill. It will make or break a company...a church...a home. The remarkable thing is we

18

have a choice everyday regarding the attitude we will embrace for that day. We cannot change our past… we cannot change the fact that people will act in a certain way. We cannot change the inevitable. The one thing we can do is play the one string we have, and that is our attitude…I am convinced that life is 10% what happens to me and 90% how I react to it. And so it is with you… we are in charge of our attitudes."

Charles Swindoll
Christian author and minister

THE MAN IN THE ARENA
"It is not the critic who counts. Not the man who points out how the strongman stumbled or where the doer of deeds could have done better. The credit belongs to the man who is actually in the arena, whose face is marred by dust and sweat and blood; who strives valiantly; who errs and comes short again and again; who knows the great enthusiasms, the great devotions; who spends himself in a worthy cause. Who, at the best, knows in the end the triumph of high achievement, and who at the worst, at least fails while daring greatly, so that his place shall never be with those timid souls who know neither victory nor defeat."

Theodore Roosevelt
First American Awarded Nobel Peace Prize
Awarded Medal of Honor
26th President of United States

"Far better is it to dare mighty things, to win glorious triumphs, even though checked by failure...than to rank with those poor spirits who neither enjoy much nor suffer

much, because they live in a gray twilight that knows not
victory nor defeat." **Theodore Roosevelt**

**THE "A" OF LEADERSHIP ALSO STANDS FOR
ACCOUNTABILITY.** True leaders are accountable for their
actions. They do not avoid responsibility; they seek it out!
Authentic leaders take responsibility regardless of the consequences.
Taking ownership of your responsibilities is freely accepting your
cross. Christ did not turn from His assigned responsibility. Jesus
embraced His Cross, therefore Christ glorified the Father and
purchased our salvation. Authentic leaders always accept
responsibility. When necessary, leaders must delegate authority, but
NEVER responsibility. The reality of it is simple; authentic leaders
accept and seek out responsibility. Many so called leaders will flee
from this responsibility of truth.

*Reflections and examination of your conscience: Is your attitude
positive... one that motivates others to strive to achieve their best?
Or do you see defeat around every corner, and settle for
mediocrity? Do you genuinely seek out responsibility, or do you
seek ways to avoid it? Do you take complete accountability for your
actions? Or do you hide behind excuses?*

*Pray: Dear Jesus teach me to receive the grace of fortitude, to shine
with Your strength; to welcome responsibility with eagerness, no
matter how daunting the circumstances, allow your humble servant
to be a beacon of hope, strength, and courage for others; to simply
and faithfully glorify God's will. Amen.*

Pray the Our Father, Hail Mary, Glory be to the Father

D= DISCIPLINE. Is the framework of success in all areas of life,
whether in the natural or supernatural order. The essence of
discipline is executing all the necessary tasks to accomplish the

mission, whether or not we enjoy doing them. When we lack discipline in prayer life, we suffer in many areas, especially spiritually. A good leader understands the essential importance of discipline in preparing for battle. Discipline is a crucial ingredient that strengthens our character, prepares us for battle, and increases our desire to please God, not our wretched self. Without discipline, we do not grow in moral or spiritual strength. We fail to reach our potential, and we fail to accomplish our missions.

Discipline provides a systematic approach to develop and prepare leaders for the rigors of command and the battles they will face. The disciplined athlete wakes up early every morning regardless of the climate conditions, completes several miles of road work, eats a proper diet, and spends the necessary hours in the gym to prepare him for battle. If leaders are not willing to endure discipline and put forth the same effort with their assigned mission, how can they expect to succeed?

> *"The discipline of the LORD, my son, disdain not; spurn not his reproof; For whom the LORD loves he reproves, and he chastises the son he favors."*
> **Proverbs 3:11-12**

> *"Endure your trials as "discipline"; God treats you as sons. For what "son" is there whom his father does not discipline? If you are without discipline, in which all have shared, you are not sons but bastards. Besides this, we have had our earthly fathers to discipline us, and we respected them. Should we not (then) submit all the more to the Father of spirits and live? They disciplined us for a short time as seemed right to them, but he does so for our benefit, in order that we may share his holiness. At the time, all discipline seems a cause not for joy*

but for pain, yet later it brings the peaceful fruit of righteousness to those who are trained by it."
Hebrews 12:7-11

How can they expect to achieve victory or survive the battle? Christ provides a clear example of discipline in prayer and obedience to the Father's will with his words and actions. Are you disciplined with living God's commandments?

Reflections and examination of your conscience: *Do you seek improvement in the areas in which you are weak? Are you disciplined in faith, prayer, regular confession, attending Mass and demonstrating genuine acts of mercy? Do you invite God into your heart daily to strengthen you?*

Pray: *Dear Jesus teach me to accept the gift of discipline with a grateful heart and willfully accept the day in and day out demands that are expected and required of me. To understand that much has been given to me and much will be required of me. That I come to love the sweetness of discipline and self-control, for the Kingdom of God; to simply and faithfully glorify God's will. Amen.*

Pray the Our Father, Hail Mary, Glory be to the Father

E= EMPOWER your subordinates by providing them with the necessary training and tools to succeed. To help them successfully accomplish their missions, it is crucial that leaders understand the importance of providing necessary training, support, and presenting clear directions to their subordinates. The Gospel is full of examples of Christ empowering the Apostles for the mission that awaited them. He communicated clear and concise objectives to them.

22

> *"Then Jesus approached and said to them, "All power in heaven and on earth has been given to me. Go, therefore, and make disciples of all nations, baptizing them in the name of the Father, and of the Son, and of the Holy Spirit, teaching them to observe all that I have commanded you. And behold, I am with you always, until the end of the age."* **Matthew 28:18-20**
> *"Jesus said to him in reply, "Blessed are you, Simon son of Jonah. For flesh and blood has not revealed this to you, but my heavenly Father. And so I say to you, you are Peter, and upon this rock I will build my church, and the gates of the netherworld shall not prevail against it. I will give you the keys to the kingdom of heaven. Whatever you bind on earth shall be bound in heaven; and whatever you loose on earth shall be loosed in heaven."* **Matthew 16:17-19**

Communication is essential to empowering your subordinates. Another essential element is providing proper authority to your men. This empowers them to accomplish their mission. Christ bestowing upon St. Peter the keys of the Church is a powerful example. Empowering the Apostles by sending the Holy Spirit is another.

Empowering your subordinates contains three essential elements:
1) Necessary and detail-oriented training geared toward the mission.
2) Clear and concise communications that have an objective, end state (task and purpose), and time line.
3) Subordinates must be given appropriate levels of authority to accomplish their assigned mission.

23

During my twenty three years in the US Army Special Forces, I witnessed several commanders and senior NCOs stifle the progress and /or potential of their subordinates because they failed to understand how to empower them. They were ineffective leaders thus the men and mission suffered.

Leadership is always about hope, willingness to sacrifice and empowering your subordinates. During the darkest hours of World War II Great Britain faced the Nazi war machine by itself. Western Europe was on the verge of total collapse. 4,700 British citizens died every month during the Nazi Luftwaffe bombing campaign. The British people were suffering greatly; during one of Winston Churchill's famous radio addresses to his fellow citizens he stated the following;

"To every man there comes in his lifetime that special moment when he is figuratively tapped on the shoulder and offered a chance to do a very special thing, unique to him and fitted to his talents; What a tragedy if that moment finds him unprepared or unqualified for the work which would be his finest hour."

Sir Winston Churchill
Prime Minster of Great Britain
World War II

Reflections and examination of your conscience: *Do you micro manage your subordinates? Do you provide them with the necessary training, tools, clear communication, authority and latitude to accomplish their assigned mission? Do they understand the mission?*

Pray: *Dear Jesus teach me to accept and understand the seven gifts of the Holy Spirit; Wisdom, Understanding, Knowledge, Counsel, Fortitude, Piety, and Fear of the Lord. That I may be a living reflection of these gifts, to faithfully radiate the Love and Mercy of*

24

Christ to those around me and under my care; to simply and faithfully glorify God's will. Amen.

Pray the Our Father, Hail Mary, Glory be to the Father

R= RECEIVE AND RESPECT INPUT. Listen to concerns from your subordinates. Leaders are good listeners! This allows you an opportunity to understand their difficulties and to provide them with a lasting solution. Listening to your men provides leaders with a two fold assessment; first an effective gauge to measure morale, second it provides a leader with an accurate evaluation... with understanding of how well his men are absorbing the knowledge he is trying to impart to them. Notice how Jesus praised the Apostles when correct and rebuked them when wrong.

In this regard, we have an example when Christ questions his disciples:

> *"Now Jesus and his disciples set out for the villages of Caesarea Philippi. Along the way he asked his disciples, "Who do people say that I am?" They said in reply, "John the Baptist, others Elijah, still others one of the prophets." And he asked them, "But who do you say that I am?" Peter said to him in reply, "You are the Messiah." Then he warned them not to tell anyone about him. He began to teach them that the Son of Man must suffer greatly and be rejected by the elders, the chief priests, the scribes, and be killed, and rise after three days. He spoke this openly. Then Peter took him aside and began to rebuke him. At this he turned around and, looking at his disciples, rebuked Peter and said, "Get behind me, Satan. You are thinking not as God does, but as human beings do."* **Mark 8:27-33**

He said to them, "But who do you say that I am?"
Simon Peter said in reply, "You are the Messiah, the
Son of the living God." Jesus said to him in reply,
"Blessed are you, Simon son of Jonah. For flesh and
blood has not revealed this to you, but my heavenly
Father. **Mathew16:15-17**

Genuinely praise your subordinates when right, and correct them when they are in error. It is crucial to understand why you must correct them at that moment. Notice Jesus did not wait for several days to correct Peter or any of the Apostles. When you wait or vacillate to deliver a correction inevitably you cloud the issue and devalue its importance.

Further how you deliver the correction is also critical. Your delivery will be based on your skill sets and your knowledge of the individual at hand. A common error with delivery is getting caught up with *"I'm right"* and *"you're wrong"* attitude. Regardless how true this may be, the message and correction will be lost on your subordinate when engaging in this type of behavior. The objective is simple, be truthful and educate your subordinate; identify the issue *(poor work performance, bad behavior, etc),* explain why this is an issue, insure your subordinate understands. Then provide clear guidance that empowers your subordinate to do the right thing. Remember focus on the solution: Identify the issue, provide an honest correction in a professional manner, **never sacrifice the truth or ethical standards**, **always strive for excellence** insure your subordinate understands, and close with proper guidance that empowers him to carry out his mission. Many times the truth will hurt. Welcome to loneliness of command.

St Paul in his Second Letter to the Corinthians was clear: Say *yes* when you mean Yes and say No when you mean *no.* Be honest, do not change the standards or sacrifice the truth, focus on

26

the issue, do not make it personal, and finally always present a clear and credible solution that provides instructions and encouragement.

During my career with the Army Special Forces there are countless examples of my men approaching me with a solution to a problem. When they provided an appropriate or credible solution, I implemented it. Good leaders listen to their men. In this regard, we have the example of the Pope seeking input from college of bishops. There is much we can learn from our men by genuinely listening to their concerns. Effective leaders encourage and create an atmosphere where their men are willing to approach them with concerns. Your subordinates will provide you with solutions to problems of which you were not aware. **In the final analysis, the leader decides which course of action to take. Always remember you make the final decision: You are ultimately responsible.**

Reflections and examination of your conscience: *Do you genuinely listen to your men's concerns and input? Do you create and foster an environment that encourages your men the desire to approach you with concerns and solutions?*

Pray: *Dear Jesus teach me to respect and love others as You love us. The grace to hear the cries, sorrows, and anguish of poor souls. Lord make me a beacon of light and hope, that shines Your Love and Mercy, to give hope where there is despair, to shine light where there is darkness, and to forgive where there is injury; to simply and faithfully glorify God's will. Amen.*

Pray the Our Father, Hail Mary, Glory be to the Father

S= SACRIFICES. Selfless service for mission and men. This is vital for leaders to understand. Leaders must never forget they work for their mislabeled "subordinates!" Each and every one of us is called to serve. Christ is our greatest example. The Creator of the universe comes to save His creatures, and allowed Himself to be crucified for their salvation. Without sacrifice, leaders cannot lead.

Jesus spoke clearly on what a leader (a good shepherd) will have to endure:

> *"I am the good shepherd. A good shepherd lays down his life for the sheep. A hired man, who is not a shepherd and whose sheep are not his own, sees a wolf coming and leaves the sheep and runs away, and the wolf catches and scatters them. This is because he works for pay and has no concern for the sheep. I am the good shepherd, and I know mine and mine know me, just as the Father knows me and I know the Father; and I will lay down my life for the sheep. I have other sheep that do not belong to this fold. These also I must lead, and they will hear my voice, and there will be one flock, one shepherd. This is why the Father loves me, because I lay down my life in order to take it up again."* **John 10:11-17**

To lead is inspiring ordinary folks to do the extraordinary, to serve a cause greater than one self. This comes with a cost. We must remember our salvation was purchased with the blood of Christ, not with glory or fame, but with the trial, suffering and rejection of Jesus. Leaders must remember this when they are confronted with their own suffering. The assigned mission and the welfare of their men come first, not their own wants or desires. It is precisely during our suffering and hardship when we inspire souls toward Christ.

> *"But what credit is there if you are patient when beaten for doing wrong? But if you are patient when you suffer for doing what is good, this is grace before God. For to this you have been called, because Christ*

28

also suffered for you, leaving you an example that you should follow in his footsteps."
1 Peter 2:20-21

All that can be said about sacrifice has been accomplished by Christ on His Cross.

"Be sober and vigilant. Your opponent the devil is prowling around like a roaring lion looking for (someone) to devour. Resist him, steadfast in faith, knowing that your fellow believers throughout the world undergo the same sufferings. The God of all grace who called you to his eternal glory through Christ (Jesus) will himself restore, confirm, strengthen, and establish you after you have suffered a little. To him be dominion forever. Amen."
1 Peter 5:8-10

YOUR ASSIGNED CROSS:

"The everlasting God has in His wisdom foreseen from eternity the cross that He now presents to you as a gift from His inmost heart. This cross He now sends you He has considered with His all-knowing eyes, understood with His divine mind, tested with His wise justice, warmed with loving arms and weighed with His own hands to see that it be not one inch too large and not one ounce too heavy for you. He has blessed it with His holy Name, anointed it with His consolation, taken one last glance at you and your courage, and then sent it to you from heaven, a special greeting from God to you, an alms of the all-merciful love of God." St. Francis de Sales

REGARDING SUFFERING:

29

"If God causes you to suffer much, it is a sign that He has great designs for you, and that He certainly intends to make you a saint. And if you wish to become a great saint, entreat Him yourself to give you much opportunity for suffering; for there is no wood better to kindle the fire of holy love than the wood of the cross, which Christ used for His own great sacrifice of boundless charity." **St. Ignatius Loyola**

Reflections and examination of your conscience: *Do you avoid your cross? Do you place your assigned mission and your men first, above your own selfish needs and wants? Or do you shrink from the hardship?*

Pray: *Dear Jesus teach me to lovingly accept and courageously carry my cross to the bitter end. May I receive the grace to persevere during the trails of this life, to always place the needs of those around me and under my care ahead of myself; to freely give and not count the cost, to labor and not seek rest, to simply and faithfully glorify God's will. Amen.*

Pray the Our Father, Hail Mary, Glory be to the Father

H= HUMILITY. Is the foundation on which the rest of leadership is built on. St. Teresa tells us humility is the acknowledgment of the Truth. Humility must be part of your life. It breeds honesty and integrity. Humility is entwined with integrity and honesty. We cannot separate the three. Leaders who fail to understand the importance of humility fail to grow spiritually. They fail in their mission and ultimately fail their men. Humility is essential for a leader's ability to discern the truth, provide proper guidance and make solid decisions.

Once again we look to Christ as our example. The birth of Jesus, the creator of the universe came as an infant, wrapped in

30

swaddling clothes and He was placed in a manger. The Shepherd came to save His sheep and the world was forever changed. God almighty in the quiet of that holy night came as an innocent child, so man could approach Him in humble trust. Jesus' humility guided His mission, motivated His Apostles, and set the standard for all of us to follow.

Humility is a hallmark of maturity and wisdom; it empowers a leader to accomplish his assigned mission. Leaders must strive to live a life of humility, honesty, and integrity. This is critical for leaders to successfully have the ability to lead and inspire men in battle.

"Whoever exalts himself will be humbled; but whoever humbles himself will be exalted." **Mathew 23:12**

"And when the chief Shepherd is revealed, you will receive the unfading crown of glory. Likewise, you younger members, be subject to the presbyters. And all of you, clothe yourselves with humility in your dealings with one another, for: "God opposes the proud but bestows favor on the humble." So humble yourselves under the mighty hand of God, that he may exalt you in due time. Cast all your worries upon him because he cares for you." **1 Peter 5:4-7**

Reflections and examination of your conscience: *Does your pride and ego lead your decisions, or does humility and love for the truth? Do you seek true humility? Or are you blinded by worldly desires and accolades? Do you abuse your position or authority? Are you practicing simple acts of humility throughout the day? Are the welfare of your men and mission placed ahead of your own needs?*

Pray: *Dear Jesus remove from my heart the ugliness of pride, ego, and selfishness. Oh merciful Jesus please fill my heart with the*

*grace of humility, longanimity, peace, charity and Your love. Holy
Mary Mother of God, all the angels and saints in heaven, please
pray for me, to the Lord Our God, that I may receive and accept the
graces to live my life as a humble servant of Christ, to simply and
faithfully glorify God's will. Amen.*

Pray the Our Father, Hail Mary, Glory be to the Father
I= INITIATIVE. Seize the day. Each day, each moment in time,
each thought, each interaction with someone is an opportunity for
initiative. When leaders fail to understand initiative, they end up
reacting to problems. Once we loose initiative, the tide of battle
swings toward the enemy. Events begin to control the actions of the
leader rather than the leader's initiative controlling the events.
Leaders anticipate problems (and identify solutions) before the
problems reach "critical mass." Initiative in action is controlling the
events surrounding your mission. When events control your every
decision and action, you have lost the initiative, and defeat will
follow in short order. Leaders do not stand by with idle hands!
They are constantly in action, constantly working, constantly in
thought with how to better serve their men and accomplish the
mission at hand.

Leaders do not rest in thought or in action. **Seizing the initiative is
crucial**; leaders must always lean forward in the foxhole.
St. Paul provides a wonderful example of initiative in his letter to
the Ephesians.

> *"Finally, draw your strength from the Lord and from
> his mighty power. Put on the armor of God so that you
> may be able to stand firm against the tactics of the
> devil. For our struggle is not with flesh and blood but
> with the principalities, with the powers, with the world
> rulers of this present darkness, with the evil spirits in
> the heavens. Therefore, put on the armor of God, that
> you may be able to resist on the evil day and, having*

32

*done everything, to hold your ground. So stand fast
with your loins girded in truth, clothed with
righteousness as a breastplate, and your feet shod in
readiness for the gospel of peace. In all circumstances,
hold faith as a shield, to quench all (the) flaming
arrows of the evil one. And take the helmet of salvation
and the sword of the Spirit, which is the word of God.
With all prayer and supplication, pray at every
opportunity in the Spirit. To that end, be watchful with
all perseverance and supplication for all the holy ones
and also for me, that speech may be given me to open
my mouth, to make known with boldness the mystery of
the gospel for which I am an ambassador in chains, so
that I may have the courage to speak as I must."*
Ephesians 6:10-20

Another wonderful example of initiative is: Christ did not wait for
the Apostles to come to him. He sought them out! He hand   picked
them. Jesus seized the initiative.

*"As he passed by the Sea of Galilee, he saw Simon
and his brother Andrew casting their nets into the sea;
they were   fishermen. Jesus said to them, "Come after
me, and I will make you fishers of men." Then they
abandoned their nets and   followed him. He walked
along a little farther and saw James, the son of
Zebedee, and his brother John. They too were in a
boat mending   their nets. Then he called them. So they
left their father Zebedee in the boat along with the
hired men and followed him. Then   they came to
Capernaum, and on the Sabbath he entered the
synagogue and taught.   The people were astonished at
his teaching, for he taught them as one having
authority and not as the scribes."* **Mark 1:16-22**

33

SIC DEVS DILEXIT MVNDVM

During the Agony of The Garden Jesus took the initiative with prayer while His Apostles slept. The actions and teachings of Jesus have forever changed the world. The Shepherd came to save His sheep.

Reflections and examination of your conscience: Do you wait to be told to accomplish a necessary task, or an action that is expected of you? Does your lack of inaction create more obstacles and difficulties? Do you find yourself overwhelmed by events? Initiative takes courage, foresight and the willingness to act. Remember choosing the easy wrong over the hard right always leads to failure.

"An error in the beginning is an error indeed."
St. Thomas Aquinas Doctor of the Church.

Pray: Dear Jesus teach me to take proper action when necessary, grant me the grace of understanding, to enlighten my mind with the light of Your divine truth. To recognize every day, every moment, every interaction, and every thought is an opportunity to glorify Your Kingdom and Your will. Oh Lord teach me Your initiative; to simply and faithfully glorify God's will. Amen.

Pray the Our Father, Hail Mary, Glory be to the Father

P= PLAN. Authentic leaders have well thought out plans drawn from their training, experience and knowledge. The importance of planning cannot be overstated. The time spent in proper planning and preparation is equally important as the actual battle itself. Without a properly drawn up plan and coupled with poor preparation of men or equipment, the outcome of the battle has already been determined before it started. A solid plan will always address the **five W's; Who, What, Why, Where and How.** This is

34

SIC DEVS DILEXIT MVNDVM

critical for every leader to truly grasp in order to achieve victory. These principles apply to all human endeavors.

A Solid Plan Will Consist Of The Following Characteristic:

1. **Prayer**   *For Guidance, Strength, and Wisdom*
2. **Patience**   *To endure, stay focused, set the example for your men*
3.   **Prepare**   <u>*Spiritual Preparation:*</u> *Fasting, Confession, attend Mass,* **and** *Pray.* <u>*Physical Preparation*</u>*: Identify what you and your men will be facing, identify objectives that must be achieved for the mission to be successful, what factors will affect men & equipment, have an honest assessment of your capabilities and your men, and prepare and train the men for the conditions they will face during battle. Do not cut corners with planning or training. How much time do you have to prepare?* ***Did you properly answer all the five Ws?***
4. **Practice**   *It never stops.*

Pray: Good leaders consistently pray everyday. They pray for the welfare of their men and their mission. During our Lord's Agony in the Garden, Jesus knew completely what awaited Him and He immersed Himself in prayer. Christ is always our best example. Leaders pray, George Washington during the frozen desolation of Valley Forge, Abraham Lincoln during the darkest hours of the Civil War, they prayed to Our Lord frequently, turning to Christ for strength, guidance and wisdom.

Saint Bede the Venerable one of the thirty three Doctors of The Church is an example of a prayer warrior. As a child he demonstrated authentic faithfulness to pray.

"When the yellow plague struck Wearmouth and Jarrow (England) in 685, only one boy and the Abbot Ceolfrid were left alive of all those at Jarrow who could chant the

35

*Office. With hardly any doubt this boy was Bede. With
the monastery cut down so drastically, Ceolfrid held
limited hours of prayer; but after one week, he could
stand it no longer, and he chanted the Office with just
the boy."*
Fr. Christopher Rengers, O.F.M. The 33 Doctors of the
Church.

With death surrounding them, the Abbot Ceolfrid and a
young boy continued to pray to God. The young boy grew to
manhood and became a priest, who wrote *The Ecclesiastical
History of the English People,* this priest would be given the title
"Father of English History" who was this young boy? St Bede a
Doctor of the Church. His devotion to prayer even when death
surrounded him is an example for all of us.

Patience: Leaders must exercise and demonstrate patience, without
it you quickly lose focus and perspective during trial and hardship.
Leaders will require patience from their men in order to be
successful.
The only way to achieve that a leader must willingly demonstrate
patience day in and day out, regarding his actions and thoughts
while the burden of command weighs upon him.

Prepare: Spiritually, Physically, and mentally. The importance to
understand and apply proper preparation in all three areas cannot be
overstated. Leaders develop well thought out plans in all three
areas, prior to a conflict striking. This preparation will carry you
through the battles that lie ahead. Pray, frequent Confession, and
always attend Mass.

When you find yourself in a whirlwind of despair and the
enemy is ferociously beating you down without mercy, turn to

36

SIC DEVS DILEXIT MVNDVM

Christ and cry out the Holy name of "Jesus!" Have faith and trust in Christ and never lose hope. Never forget the profound love the Blessed Mother has for her Son, she will always lead you to her Son. Ask Mary to pray for you, ask her to place your intentions in her Immaculate heart. And always take ACTION! Remember place into action your prepared battle drills. Seize the initiative. Do not relinquish it to the enemy!

Plans and battle drills are based on the leaders training, experience and knowledge. They prepare themselves and their men for battle. Leaders persevere under hardship; they do not wilt under the first signs of trial or suffering. They practice and train hard for the fight they will encounter; they focus their training on specific areas in which he and his men will find themselves during battle. **Always address and properly answer the five Ws; Who, What, Why, Where and How.**

Authentic leaders never cut corners regarding preparedness, demanding training, and they never compromise on the truth. Before Christ embarked on his ministry, He prepared by fasting and praying for forty days and nights in the desert. He prepared His Apostles, and He persevered to the bitter end. The Passion, Death and Resurrection of Christ, triumphs over sin and death; the gates of heaven are open. Thanks be to God.

Practice: Leaders along with their men practice….practice….. and practice, it never ends. The focus is their battle drills, with a determined understanding what the mission is and what is at stake. You are always honing your skill sets, there is no rest. We having a saying in the Army *"the more you sweat in training, the less you bleed on the battle field."* Take these words to heart, many men have lost their lives or were seriously wounded due to the lack of preparation. Failure to train hard and failure to train to standard will put your men and mission in jeopardy.

SIC DEVS DILEXIT MVNDVM

SIC DEVS DILEXIT MVNDVM

Reflections and examination of your conscience: Do you pray to Christ for strength, guidance, and wisdom? Do you ask Jesus to fill your heart with His peace, perseverance and patience? Do you prepare yourself and the men under your charge for the battle at hand? Do you pray genuinely for your men? Do you faithfully execute and practice your battle plans?

Pray: Dear Jesus teach me to pray with a servant's heart, to receive the graces of peace and patience; to preserve during the struggles and hardship of this life, to properly prepare my men for the task ahead of us. Dear Lord grant me the desire to be a living example of Your ten commandments, that those around me and under my care clearly see the truth of Your words. The desire to embrace the three theological virtues of faith, hope and charity; and to simply and faithfully glorify God's will. Amen.

Pray the Our Father, Hail Mary, Glory be to the Father

EPILOGUE

The Ten Fundamentals of Leadership are essential for any leader to succeed in his or her assigned mission. Every day, every moment, every interaction is an opportunity to glorify Christ. Whether you're a parent, teacher, CEO, military officer, priest, or brick layer, we are all called to lead in some form or another. Failure to understand and apply these ten fundamentals results in ineffective leaders. We witness the results in every segment of society. Outside forces and events end up controlling individuals and the situation at hand. Authentic leadership can and will be lonely. Leaders sacrifice themselves for their men and the mission. Christ is the greatest example. Are you willing to pick up your cross and follow Christ?

SIC DEVS DILEXIT MVNDVM

      I find myself compelled to write this document as testimony to the Lord's mercy and love for sinners. My sins are vast and numerous. The Lord's mercy has humbled me. I simply desire to serve and glorify Christ. The Lord will strengthen us for the specific mission He's given to each of us. Shouldering your cross and following Christ is never easy, it never was meant to be easy, yet this is what we are all called to do. The highest human triumph is to serve Christ Crucified with all your heart, mind, soul and strength. The conscious action to submit oneself to Christ allows the individual to receive the transforming grace of the Holy Spirit. The humbled soul becomes a witness to the fruits of the Holy Spirit radiating God's Mercy and Love for sinners.

      Each and every one of us is assigned a specific mission, from the beginning of eternity, God entrusted you with a specific mission that only you can accomplish. The Blessed Mother's *fiat* is a magnificent example. Our act of the will is a precious gift. When we faithfully and obediently submit ourselves to Christ, we become an instrument of peace and mercy guided by the hands of God. Just as infinite graces flow from the Passion of Christ so will graces from heaven flow through your carrying the cross of leadership. Many souls will be led to Christ. Endure the weight of your cross, for it glorifies Christ. All of us, whether we choose to or not, are called to lead, to lead others toward Christ.

      Who among us will answer the call? Who among us will pick up and labor under the weight, the ridicule, the hardship, and the glory of carrying your cross towards Christ Crucified?

† MSG Michael Cutone

CATHOLIC PRAYERS, WRITINGS, & ARTWORK: TO NOURISH, STRENGTHEN, AND GUIDE LEADERS

The Holy Trinity

APOSTLES CREED
(Profession of faith)

I believe in God the Father Almighty,
Creator of Heaven and earth;
I believe in Jesus Christ,
His only Son, our Lord,
He was conceived by the Holy Spirit
and born of the Virgin Mary.
He suffered under Pontius Pilate,
was crucified, died, and was buried.
He descended to the dead.
On the third day He rose again.
He ascended into Heaven
and is seated at the right hand of the Father.
He will come again to judge the living and the dead.
I believe in the Holy Spirit,
the Holy Catholic Church,
the communion of Saints,
the forgiveness of sins,
the resurrection of the body,
and the life everlasting.
Amen.

OUR FATHER
Our Father, who art in heaven, hallowed be thy name;
thy kingdom come; thy will be done on earth as it is in heaven.
Give us this day our daily bread; and forgive us our trespasses
as we forgive those who trespass against us; and lead us
not into temptation, but deliver us from evil. Amen.

HAIL MARY

Hail, Mary! Full of grace, The Lord is with thee;
Blessed are thou among women, And blessed is the fruit of thy
womb, Jesus. Holy Mary, Mother of God, Pray for us sinners, now,
and at the hour of our death. Amen.

GLORY BE TO THE FATHER

Glory be to the Father, and to the Son,
and to the Holy Spirit: As it was in the beginning,
is now, and ever shall be, world without end. Amen.

FATIMA PRAYER

O My Jesus, forgive us our sins,
save us from the fires of hell,
lead all souls to Heaven,
especially those most in need of Thy mercy.

ST. MICHAEL ARCHANGEL PRAYER

St. Michael the Archangel, defend us in battle. Be our safeguard
against the wickedness and snares of the devil. May God rebuke
him, we humbly pray; and do you, O Prince of the heavenly host, by
the power of God cast into hell Satan and all the evil spirits who
wander through the world seeking the ruin of souls. Amen.

A PRAYER TO REBUKE SATAN

Heavenly Father, I ask You in the name, and through the Blood of
Your Divine Son, to rebuke Satan for taking captive that which
belongs to You. I ask Jesus to place His Crown of thorns around
(Name the person) so that those with wrong influences will lose
interest and depart. Mary Mother of Jesus, place your mantle of love
around, (your son and/or your daughter.) Amen

St. Michael, protect them.

SIC DEVS DILEXIT MVNDVM

A Short History of the Prayer of St. Michael the Archangel

The Prayer of St. Michael the Archangel goes back to the late 19th Century. In 1884, Pope Leo XIII was finishing Mass and was walking away from the Tabernacle when he collapsed. Those that were at the mass surrounded him and when a pulse could not be found, he was thought to be dead. The Pope then "came to", having collapsed in a state of ecstasy. He then related what he had experienced. From in front of the Tabernacle, he had heard a confrontation between Jesus and Satan. Satan was bragging to Jesus that if he had enough time and enough power, he could destroy the Church.

Jesus asked him "How much time and how much power?" Satan replied he would need a century and more influence over those that would give themselves to him. Jesus said "So be it." The 20th Century is the century that was given to him to test the world. The Pope was quite shaken having heard this and went immediately to write the Laentein. Exorcism Prayer, of which the Prayer of St. Michael the Archangel is the short version. Pope Leo XIII also knew that the Rosary would be the weapon that would defeat Satan. He went on to write 13 Encyclicals on the Rosary. (*Provided by Celia G. Lazaro, as e-mailed to her by Roberta Ann Marziani*)

SIC DEVS DILEXIT MVNDVM

PRAYER TO DEFEAT THE WORK OF SATAN

O Divine Eternal Father, in union with your Divine Son and the Holy Spirit, and through the Immaculate Heart of Mary, I beg You to destroy the Power of your greatest enemy - the evil spirits. Cast them into the deepest recesses of hell and chain them there forever! Take possession of your Kingdom which You have created and which is rightfully yours. Heavenly Father, give us the reign of the Sacred Heart of Jesus and the Immaculate Heart of Mary. I repeat this prayer out of pure love for You with every beat of my heart and with every breath I take. Amen

Imprimatur, March 1973, †Richard H. Ackerman, Bishop of Covington

Photograph taken by MSG Michael Cutone

THE ANGELUS

The Angelus is traditionally recited morning (6:00 a.m.), noon and evening (6:00 p.m.) throughout the year except during Paschal time, when the Regina Coeli is recited instead.

V. The Angel of the Lord declared unto Mary.
R. And she conceived of the Holy Spirit.
Pray a *Hail Mary,*
V. Behold the handmaid of the Lord.
R. Be it done unto me according to thy word.
Pray a *Hail Mary,*

V. And the Word was made Flesh.
R. And dwelt among us.
Pray a *Hail Mary,*
V. Pray for us, O Holy Mother of God.
R. That we may be made worthy of the promises of Christ.

The Angelus is traditionally recited morning (6:00 a.m.), noon and evening (6:00 p.m.) throughout the year except during Paschal time, then the Regina Coeli is recited instead.

LET US PRAY: Pour forth, we beseech Thee, O Lord, Thy grace into our hearts, that we to whom the Incarnation of Christ Thy Son was made known by the message of an angel, may by His Passion and Cross be brought to the glory of His Resurrection. Through the same Christ Our Lord. Amen.

Indulgence by Pope Benedict XIII, September 14, 1724 AD

TRINITARIAN PRAYER

God, our Father, I offer You my day. I offer You my prayers, thoughts, words, actions, joys, and sufferings in union with Your Son Jesus Christ, Who continues to offer Himself in the Eucharist for the salvation of the world.

May the Holy Spirit, Who guided Jesus, be my guide and my strength today so that I may witness to Your love. With Mary, the mother of our Lord and of the Church, I pray especially for this month's intentions as proposed by the Holy Father. Amen.

PRAYERS AND WORDS OF ENCOURAGEMENT
ST. IGNATIUS LOYOLA

ANIMA CHRISTI
"Soul of Christ, sanctify me
Body of Christ, save me
Blood of Christ, inebriate me
Water from Christ's side, wash me
Passion of Christ, strengthen me
O good Jesus, hear me
Within Thy wounds hide me
Suffer me not to be separated from Thee
From the malicious enemy defend me
In the hour of my death call me
And bid me come unto Thee.
That with Thy saints I may praise Thee
Forever and ever. Amen"

> ***St. Ignatius Loyola***
> *Former Spanish soldier*
> *Founder of Catholic Jesuit order*

GLORIFY GOD
"Do not let any occasion of gaining merit pass without taking care to draw some spiritual profit from it; as, for example, from a sharp word which someone may say to you; from an act of obedience imposed against your will; from an opportunity which may occur to humble yourself, or to practice charity, sweetness, and patience. All of these occasions are gain for you, and you should seek to procure them; and at the close of that day, when the greatest number of them have come to you, you should go to rest most cheerful and pleased, as the merchant does on the day when he had had most chance for making money; for on that day business has prospered with him."

> ***St. Ignatius Loyola***

"There are very few people who realize what God would make of them if they abandoned themselves into his hands, and let themselves be formed by his grace."   ***St. Ignatius Loyola***

Surrender

"Take, O Lord, and receive my entire liberty, my memory, my understanding and my whole will. All that I am and all that I possess You have given me: I surrender it all to You to be disposed of according to Your will. Give me only Your love and Your grace; with these I will be rich enough, and will desire nothing more. Amen"   ***St. Ignatius Loyola***

Prayer for Generosity

"Lord, teach me to be generous.
Teach me to serve you as you deserve;
to give and not to count the cost,
to fight and not to heed the wounds,
to toil and not to seek for rest,
to labor and not to ask for reward,
save that of knowing that I do your will. Amen"
     St. Ignatius Loyola

Regarding Suffering

"If God causes you to suffer much, it is a sign that He has great designs for you, and that He certainly intends to make you a saint. And if you wish to become a great saint, entreat Him yourself to give you much opportunity for suffering; for there is no wood better to kindle the fire of holy love than the wood of the cross, which Christ used for His own great sacrifice of boundless charity."

     St. Ignatius Loyola

BATTLE LINES

"The picture. A great plain, comprising the entire Jerusalem district, where is the supreme Commander-in-Chief of the forces of good, Christ our Lord: another plain near Babylon, where Lucifer is, at the head of the enemy." *St. Ignatius Loyola*

ST. IGNATIUS AND THE JESUITS

May 1521 Ignatius (*Ignacio López de Loyola*) a thirty year old Spanish military officer found himself leading the defense at the Pampeluna garrison which was under siege by French forces. This battle would prove to be a turning point in the young officer's life. While the French were laying siege on the garrison, a cannon ball passed through Ignatius' legs. Tearing open the left calf and shattering the right lower leg along with any hope of Spanish victory that day. During his extensive and painful recovery at his home in Loyola, Ignatius convinced the doctors to re-break his leg and reset the bone all without anesthesia. While his leg was healing a portion of bone was protruding from the lower leg. He requested the doctors to saw this piece of bone off! Ignatius endured all these pains with no objection. His right leg never did heal properly. During his lengthy recovery, Ignatius requested romance novels or knight tales to pass his time while in bed. Providence would offer something a great deal different. Ignatius was given books on the Life of Christ and Lives of The Saints.

Desperate he began to read and the more he read, thoughts of imitating the lives of the saints poured through his mind and soul. He began to recognize serving Christ and being a Christian, is a form of warfare. The battlefield is no longer a war torn country side, rather the field of battle rages in the souls of men!

The conversion of Ignatius embarked in full flight. Once again the soldier decided he would fight. This time Ignatius would serve under a new commander and new army, Christ and His Catholic Church. His conversion would eventually lead to establishing a new order within the Church called The Society of Jesus. They were called Jesuits by the Protestants and over time the name was embraced by the order. This new order within Catholic Church would play a critical role with defending and upholding the Doctrine of the Faith during the Protestant Reformation *(deformation, I believe, is more accurate)*.

The Jesuits successfully spread the *G*ospel to South America, India, Japan, and even parts of China. They established Catholic Universities throughout the world; the early Jesuits were de facto Special Forces of the Catholic Church. They operated in small teams of highly trained priests that deployed and labored under austere conditions. The Jesuits learned the indigenous language, culture, history, and suffered alongside the very souls they were teaching and leading. Their approach was extremely effective, enabling them to teach, train, and lead tens of thousands of indigenous people to the fullness of truth, Christ and His Catholic Church. All *"for the greater glory of God"* became the Jesuit motto. **Ad Majorem Dei Gloriam!**

RANGERS LEAD THE WAY!

The accomplishments of the early Jesuits are truly heroic; their leadership played a significant role within church history. Another example of heroic leadership is the US Army Rangers at Omaha beach during Normandy. On 6 June 1944 General Norm

SIC DEVS DILEXIT MVNDVM

Cota landed on Omaha beach with the second wave about one hour after H-Hour. He landed with 116th Infantry Regiment of the 29th Division. His landing craft was under heavy enemy machine gun and mortar fire. Three soldiers from his landing craft were immediately killed as they landed on sector Dog White of Omaha beach. General Cota was one of the highest ranking officers on the beach that day. Known for taking charge and motivating men a famous quote is credited to him on that fateful day. While on the beach under severe enemy fire General Cota asked Major Max Schneider, commander of the 5th Ranger Battalion, "What outfit is this?" Someone yelled back "5th Rangers!" General Cota replied **"Well, *(expletive)* then, Rangers, lead the way!"** "Rangers lead the way" became the motto of the US Army Rangers.. The Rangers did indeed lead the way on Omaha beach. With great cost to themselves fighting under intensive enemy fire the Rangers broke through the sea wall and barbed wire entanglements creating a gap to exploit on the beach head. Troops could finally maneuver off that deadly beach and flow inland. The breach the Rangers created was a crucial turning point during the battle and probably saved hundreds if not thousands of lives that day.

CATHOLICS LEAD THE WAY!

Several hundred years earlier the Jesuits displayed the same heroic virtue as the Rangers on Omaha beach. During the Protestant Reformation the Catholic Church was being viciously attacked from within the church, outside the church and from state powers. Certainly during this time period there were obvious issues the church had to address *i.e.* selling of indulgences and clerical abuses. The church desperately needed capable priests that were highly educated, leaders of men, accomplished teachers that would spread the Catholic faith and vigorously defend the Doctrine of the Faith. Enter the Jesuits. They would play a critical role during the Counter Reformation, defending the Doctrine of the Faith and excelling as force multipliers for the church. They were the "Green Berets" of the Catholic Church during this period. The early Jesuits were sent where Catholics lost their faith and they proved to be incredible force multipliers. St. Canisius is a fine example:

> *"The general effect of Canisius' work was immense. He turned the course of history. In each of the great colleges he built there were up to a thousand students. He was the first Jesuit to enter Poland. By 1600, there were 466 Jesuits there. When he entered Germany in 1550, he entered with 2 Jesuits as his companions. When he left it over 30 years later there were 1,111 Jesuits at work in the country."* **Christopher Hollis,** The Jesuits: A History.

The battle field has not changed. The enemy continues to attack from within and outside the church. All Catholics must understand whether religious or laity, authentic Catholic teaching must lead the way! The early Jesuits provide an excellent example of work ethic, superior teaching, and the courage to defend and uphold the Doctrine of the Faith. Their service to God is profoundly inspirational and a wonderful example for all Christians.

† MSG Michael Cutone

To further illustrate the remarkable achievements of the early Jesuits; St. Francis Xavier, one of the seven founding members of The Society of Jesus, is considered second only to St. Paul the Apostle regarding missionary accomplishments.

> *"It is truly a matter of wonder that one man in the short space of ten years (6 May, 1542 - 2 December, 1552) could have visited so many countries, traversed so many seas, preached the Gospel to so many nations, and converted so many infidels. The incomparable apostolic zeal. which animated him, and the stupendous miracles. which God. wrought through him, explain this marvel, which has no equal elsewhere."* **Catholic Encyclopedia**
> http://www.newadvent.org/cathen/06233b.htm

LOVE OF GOD

I love You, O my God, and my only desire is to love You until the last breath of my life. I love You, O my infinitely lovable God, and I would rather die loving You, than live without loving You. I love You, Lord and the only grace I ask is to love You eternally....My God, if my tongue cannot say in every moment that I love You, I want my heart to repeat it to You as often as I draw breath. Amen"

St John Vianney

BODY OF CHRIST, SAVE ME!

Body of Christ, save me! Save me from my great arch-enemy, my weak and faltering self. Save me from all greed of money, of power, and of praise. Save me from thirst for pleasure, worldly show, and midnight revelry. Save me from betraying You, Dear Lord, in thought, or in word, or in deed. Amen

It is said that the Devil told St. John Vianney, *"If there were three such priests as you, my kingdom would be ruined."*
"St. Vianney, a priest, so devoted to God, he spent hours in front of the blessed Sacrament or hearing confessions, he barely had a moment to sleep, he often went days without eating, and when he did eat, it was a boiled potato or a piece of hard bread.. To priests and seminary students do not hesitate but quickly run and obtain readings regarding the life of St. John Vianney! A remarkable priest who lived heroic virtue every day, a true servant of Christ, an example for all Christians." *† MSG Michael Cutone*

"In his assignment as parish priest of Ars, St. John achieved something which many priests would like to have done, but which is scarcely granted to any. Not over night, but little by little, the tiny hamlet underwent a change. The people of Ars were unable to remain aloof for long from the grace which radiated from the remarkable personality of their priest. When a man attacks inveterate disorders and popular vices, he challenges opposition. St. John was not unprepared – he knew the enemy would raise his head."

"If a priest determined not to lose his soul," he exclaimed, "so soon as any disorder arises in the parish, he must trample underfoot all human considerations as well as the fear of the contempt and hatred of his people. He must not allow anything to bar his way in the discharge of duty, even were he certain of being murdered on coming down from the pulpit. A pastor who wants to do his duty must keep his sword in hand at all times. Did not St. Paul himself write to the faithful of Corinth: 'I most gladly will spend and be spent myself for your souls, although loving you more, I be loved less." **St John Vianney**

<u>**The Secret of His Holiness – A lesson for Priest and Parents**</u>
http://olrl.org/lives/vianney.shtml

SIC DEVS DILEXIT MVNDVM

PRAYER TO OBTAIN FINAL PERSEVERANCE

"Eternal Father, I humbly adore Thee, and thank Thee for having created me, and for having redeemed me through Jesus Christ. I thank Thee most sincerely for having made me a Christian, by giving me the true faith, and by adopting me as Thy son, in the sacrament of baptism. I thank Thee for having, after the numberless sins I had committed, waited for my repentance, and for having pardoned (as I humbly hope) all the offences which I have offered to Thee, and for which I am now sincerely sorry, because they have been displeasing to Thee, who art infinite goodness. I thank Thee for having preserved me from so many relapses, of which I would have been guilty if Thou hadst not protected me. But my enemies still continue, and will continue till death, to combat against me, and to endeavor to make me their slave. If Thou dost not constantly guard and succor me with thy aid, I, a miserable creature, shall return to sin, and shall certainly lose Thy grace. I beseech Thee, then, for the love of Jesus Christ, to grant me holy perseverance unto death. Jesus, Thy Son, has promised that Thou wilt grant whatsoever we ask in his name. Through the merits, then, of Jesus Christ, I beg, for myself and for all the just, the grace never again to be separated from Thy love, but to love Thee forever, in time and eternity. Mary, Mother of God, pray to Jesus for me."

St. Alphonsus Maria de Liguori

Renewing Baptism Promise: Read during Easter Vigil Mass
Priest: Do you reject Satan? **Response:** I do. **P.** And all his works? **R.** I do. **P.** And all his empty promises? **R.** I do. **P.** Do you believe in God, the Father Almighty, creator of heaven and earth? **R.** I do. **P.** Do you believe in Jesus Christ, his only Son, our Lord, who was born of the Virgin Mary was crucified, died, and was buried, rose from the dead, and is now seated at the right hand of the Father? **R.** I do. **P.** Do you believe in the Holy Spirit, the holy Catholic Church, the communion of saints, the forgiveness of sins, the resurrection of the body, and life everlasting? **R.** I do.

SIC DEVS DILEXIT MVNDVM 54

P. God, the all-powerful Father of our Lord Jesus Christ has given us a new birth by water and the Holy Spirit, and forgiven all our sins. May he also keep us faithful to our Lord Jesus Christ for ever and ever. **R.** Amen.

PRAYER BEFORE A Crucifix

Look down upon me, good and gentle Jesus, while before Your face I humbly kneel, and with burning soul pray and beseech You to fix deep in my heart lively sentiments of faith, hope, and charity, true contrition for my sins, and a firm purpose of amendment; while I contemplate with great love and tender pity Your five wounds, pondering over them within me, and calling to mind the words which, long ago, David the prophet spoke in Your own person concerning You, my Jesus: "They have pierced My hands and My feet; they have numbered all My bones."

"A plenary indulgence is granted on each Friday of Lent and Passiontide to the faithful who, after Communion, piously recite the above prayer before an image of Christ crucified; on other days of the year the indulgence is partial." --Enchiridion of Indulgences, No. 22 / Indulgenced by Pope Benedict XIV (1740-1758)

MY DAILY OFFERING

Jesus, through the Immaculate Heart of Mary, I offer You my prayers, works, joys, and sufferings of this day in union with the Holy Sacrifice of the Mass throughout the world. I offer them for all the intentions of Your Sacred Heart: the salvation of souls, reparation for sin, and the reunion of all Christians. I offer them for the intentions of our bishops and of all Apostles of Prayer, and in particular for those recommended by our Holy Father this month. Amen.

PRAYER OF ST. GERTRUDE THE GREAT

Eternal Father, I offer Thee the most Precious Blood of Thy Divine Son, Jesus, in union with the Masses said throughout the world today, for all the Holy souls in Purgatory, for sinners everywhere, for sinners in the Universal Church, Those in my own home and within my family. Amen.

Our Lord told St. Gertrude the Great that this prayer would release 1,000 souls from Purgatory each time it is said. The prayer was later extended to include living sinners as well. The Approval and Recommendation does NOT include this extension.

APPROVAL AND RECOMMENDATION (sqd.) M. Cardinal Pahiarca at Lisbon, Portugal, on March 4, 1936

PRAYER TO SAINT JOSEPH

O ST. JOSEPH, whose protection is so great, so strong, so prompt before the throne of God, I place in thee all my interests and desires. O St. Joseph, assist me by thy powerful intercession and obtain for me all spiritual blessings through thy foster Son, Jesus Christ Our Lord, so that, having engaged here below thy heavenly power, I may offer thee my thanksgiving and homage. O St. Joseph, I never weary contemplating thee and Jesus asleep in thine arms. I dare not approach while He reposes near thy heart. press Him in my name and kiss His fine head for me, and ask Him to return the kiss when I draw my dying breath. St. Joseph, Patron of departing souls, pray for me. Amen.

"This prayer (St. Joseph Prayer) was found in the fiftieth year of our Lord and Savior Jesus Christ. In 1505, it was sent from the pope to Emperor Charles when he was going into battle. Whoever shall read this prayer or hear it or keep it about themselves shall never die a sudden death or be drowned, nor shall poison take effect on them—neither shall they fall into the hands of the enemy or be burned in any fire or be overpowered in battle. Say for nine mornings for anything you desire. It has never been known to fail, provided that the request is for one's spiritual benefit or for those whom we are praying for."

SIC DEVS DILEXIT MVNDVM

THE THREE THEOLOGICAL VIRTUES

1. ACT OF FAITH: O MY GOD, I firmly believe that Thou art one God in Three Divine Persons, Father, Son and Holy Ghost. I believe that Thy Divine Son became Man, and died for our sins, and that He will come to judge the living and the dead. I believe these and all the truths which the Holy Catholic Church teaches, because Thou hast revealed them, Who canst neither deceive nor be deceived.

2. ACT OF HOPE: O MY GOD, relying on Thy almighty power and infinite mercy and promises, I hope to obtain pardon of my sins, the help of Thy grace, and Life Everlasting, through the merits of Jesus Christ, my Lord and Redeemer.

3. ACT OF CHARITY: O MY GOD, I love Thee above all things, with my whole heart and soul, because Thou art all-good and worthy of all love. I love my neighbor as myself for the love of Thee. I forgive all who have injured me, and ask pardon of all whom I have injured.

AN ACT OF CONTRITION: O my God, I am heartily sorry for all my sins because of them I deserve the eternal pains of hell, but most of all because I have offended Thee my God who art all-good and deserving of all my love. I firmly resolve with the help of Thy grace to confess my sins, to do penance, to avoid the proximate occasion of sin and never to sin anymore. Amen.

THE GOLDEN ARROW: May the most holy, most sacred, most adorable, most mysterious and unutterable Name of God be always praised, blessed, loved, adored and glorified, in heaven, on earth and under the earth, by all the creatures of God, and by the Sacred Heart of Our Lord Jesus Christ in the Most Holy Sacrament of the Altar. Amen. *The Golden Arrow was revealed by Our Lord Jesus Christ to a Carmelite Nun sr. Mary of St. Peter of Tours in 1843. Jesus said: "This Golden Arrow will wound My Heart delightfully, and heal the wounds inflicted by blasphemy.*

May God the Father who made us bless us. May God the Son send His healing among us. May God the Holy Spirit move within us and give us eyes to see with, ears to hear with, and hands that your work might be done. May we walk and preach the word of God to all. May the angel of peace watch over us and lead us at last by God's grace to the Kingdom. Amen.
St. Dominic

PRAYER FOR COURAGE

Dear God, give me courage, for perhaps I lack it more than anything else. I need courage before men against their threats and against their seductions. I need courage to bear unkindness, mockery, contradiction. I need courage to fight against the devil, against terrors and troubles, temptations, attractions, darkness and false lights, against tears, depression, and above all fear. I need Your help, dear God. Strengthen me with Your love and Your grace. Console me with Your blessed Presence and grant me the courage to persevere until I am with You forever in heaven. Amen.

SIC DEVS DILEXIT MVNDVM

PRAYER FOR DAILY NEGLECTS

Eternal Father, I offer Thee the Sacred Heart of Jesus, with all its love, all its sufferings and all its merits.

First --- To expiate all the sins I have committed this day and during all my life. Glory be…to the Father..

Second --- To purify the good I have done poorly this day and during all my life. Glory be…to the Father..

Third --- To supply for the good I ought to have done, and that I have neglected this day and all my life. Glory be to the Father…, Amen

A Poor Clare, who just died, appeared to her Abbess who was praying for her, and said to her: "I went straight to heaven, for, by means of this prayer, recited every evening, I paid all my debts."

This prayer is not meant to replace confession.

THREE VERY BEAUTIFUL PRAYERS

Which are very useful to a dying person, and should be prayed often as an act of mercy. There once was a Pope in Rome who was surrounded by many sins. The Lord God struck him with a fatal illness. When he saw that he was dying he summoned Cardinals, Bishops and learned persons and said to them: "My dear friends! What comfort can you give me now that I must die, and when I deserve eternal damnation for my sins?" No one answered him. One of thorn, a pious curate named John, said: "Father, why do you doubt the Mercy of God?" The Pope replied: 'What comfort can you give me now that I must die and fear that I'll be damned for my sins?" John replied: "I'll read three prayers over you; I hope you'll be comforted and that you'll obtain Mercy from God". The Pope was unable to say more. The curate and all those present knelt and said an Our Father, then the following Prayers:

SIC DEVS DILEXIT MVNDVM

1. Prayer: Lord Jesus Christ! Thou Son of God and Son of the Virgin Mary, God and Man, Thou who in fear sweated blood for us on the Mount of Olives in order to bring peace, and to offer Thy Most Holy Death to God Thy Heavenly Father for the salvation of this dying person ...... If it be, however, that by his sins he merits eternal damnation, then may it be deflected from him. This, 0 Eternal Father through Our Lord Jesus Christ, Thy Dear Son, Who liveth and reigneth in union with The Holy Spirit now and forever. Amen.

2. Prayer: Lord Jesus Christ! Thou Who meekly died on the trunk of the Cross for us, submitting Thy Will completely to Thy Heavenly Father in order to bring peace and to offer Thy most Holy Death to Thy Heavenly Father in order to free ......(this person) ... and to hide from him what he has earned with his sins; grant this 0 Eternal Father! Through Our Lord Jesus Thy Son, Who liveth and reigneth with Thee in union with the Holy Spirit now and forever. Amen.

3. Prayer: Lord Jesus Christ! Thou Who remained silent to speak through the mouths of the Prophets: I have drawn Thee to me through Eternal Love, which Love drew Thee from Heaven into the body of The Virgin, which Love drew Thee from the body of The Virgin into the valley of this needful world, which Love kept Thee 33 years in this world, and as a sign of Great Love, Thou hast given Thy Holy Body as True Food and Thy Holy Blood as True Drink, as a sign of Great Love, Thou has consented to be a prisoner and to be led from one judge to another and as a sign of Great Love Thou hast consented to be condemned to death, and hast consented to die and to be buried and truly risen, and appeared to Thy Holy Mother and all the Holy Apostles, and as a sign of Great Love Thou hast ascended, under Thy own Strength and Power, and sitteth at the Right Hand of God Thy Heavenly Father, and Thou has sent Thy Holy Spirit into the hearts of Thy Apostles and the hearts of all who hope and believe in Thee. Through Thy Sign of Eternal Love, open

Heaven today and take this dying person .... and all his sins into the Realm of Thy Heavenly Father, that he may reign with Thee now and forever. Amen.

Meanwhile, the Pope died the curate persevered to the third hour, then the Pope appeared to him in body and comforting him; his countenance as brilliant as the sun, his clothes as white as snow, and he said: "My dear brother! Whereas I was supposed to be a child of damnation I've become a child of happiness. As you recited the first Prayer many of my sins fell from me as rain from Heaven, and as you recited the second Prayer I was purified, as a goldsmith purifies gold in a hot fire.
I was still further purified as you recited the third Prayer. Then I saw Heaven open and the Lord Jesus standing on the Right Hand of God the Father Who said to me: "'Come, all thy sins are forgiven thee, you'll be and remain in the Realm of My Father forever. Amen!"

With these words my soul separated from my body and the Angels of God led it to Eternal Joy. As the curate heard this he said: "O Holy Father! I can't tell these things to anyone, for they won't believe me." Then the Pope said: "Truly I tell thee, the Angel of God stands with me and has written the prayers in letters of gold for the consolement of all sinners.

The person who hears them read, he won't die an unhappy death also in whose house they will be read. Therefore take these prayers and carry them into St. Peter's Basilica and lay them in the Chapel named the Assumption of Mary, for certain consolation. The person who will be near death, who reads them or hears them read gains 400 years indulgence for the days he was supposed to suffer in Purgatory because of his guilt. Also who reads this prayer or hears it read, the hour of his death shall be revealed to him. Amen!

PRAYER TO CONTINUE TO FIGHT FOR GOD

"Lord, if your people still have need of my services, I will not avoid the toil. Your will be done. I have fought the good fight long enough. Yet if you bid me continue to hold the battle line in defense of your camp, I will never beg to be excused from failing strength. I will do the work you entrust to me. While you command, I will fight beneath your banner. Amen"

St Martin of Tours,
Former Roman Cavalry Officer
Hermit, became Bishop of Tours

PRAYER FOR PEACE

"Lord, make me an instrument of your peace, Where there is hatred, let me sow love; where there is injury, pardon; where there is doubt, faith; where there is despair, hope; where there is darkness, light; where there is sadness, joy;

O Divine Master, grant that I may not so much seek to be consoled as to console; to be understood as to understand; to be loved as to love. For it is in giving that we receive; it is in pardoning that we are pardoned; and it is in dying that we are born to eternal life. Amen"

St. Francis of Assisi
Former party animal, Mercenary, POW
Founder of Franciscan Order

To learn more about this incredible saint visit the following links:
http://www.ewtn.com/library/mary/francis.htm
http://www.newadvent.org/cathen/06221a.htm

SIC DEVS DILEXIT MVNDVM

Prayer for The Unborn

Heavenly Father, in Your love for us, protect against the wickedness of the devil, those helpless little ones to whom You have given the gift of life. Touch with pity the hearts of those women pregnant in our world today who are not thinking of motherhood. Help them to see that the child they carry is made in Your image, as well as theirs, made for eternal life. Dispel their fear of selfishness and give them true womanly hearts to love their babies and give them birth and all the needed care that a mother can give. We ask this through Jesus Christ, Your Son, Our Lord Who lives and reigns with You and the Holy Spirit, One God, forever and ever. Amen.

By Father Angelus Shaughnessy,
Order of Friars Minor, Capuchin

Spirtual Adoption Prayer

Jesus, Mary and Joseph, I love you very much. I beg you to spare the life of [baby's name] the unborn baby that I have spiritually adopted who is in danger of abortion. *By Archbishop Fulton Sheen*

"Dear Lord, teach parents day by day to love and care, for their children, as You love and care for us. Amen" *† MSG Michael Cutone*

Jesus, Mary I love you. Save souls.

NOVENA OF THE MIRACULOUS MEDAL

Photograph taken by MSG Michael Cutone

O Immaculate Virgin Mary, Mother of Our Lord Jesus and our Mother, penetrated with the most lively confidence in your all-powerful and never-failing intercession, manifested so often through the Miraculous Medal, we your loving and trustful children implore you to obtain for us the graces and favors we ask during this novena, if they be beneficial to our immortal souls, and the souls for whom we pray.

(You're Petition)

You know, O Mary, how often our souls have been the sanctuaries of your Son who hates iniquity. Obtain for us then a deep hatred of sin and that purity of heart which will attach us to God alone so that our every thought, word and deed may tend to His greater glory. Obtain for us also a spirit of prayer and self-denial that we may recover by penance what we have lost by sin and at length attain to that blessed abode where you are the Queen of angels and of men. Amen.

Visit the following web site for a through history and significance behind Miraculous Medal. ***http://www.amm.org/medal.asp***

SIC DEVS DILEXIT MVNDVM

PRAYER TO THE SHOULDER WOUND OF CHRIST

O Loving Jesus, meek Lamb of God, I, a miserable sinner, salute and worship the most Sacred Wound of Thy Shoulder on which Thou didst bear Thy heavy Cross, which so tore Thy flesh and laid bare Thy Bones as to inflict on Thee an anguish greater than any other wound of Thy Most Blessed Body. I adore Thee, O Jesus most sorrowful; I praise and glorify Thee, and give Thee thanks for this most sacred and painful Wound, beseeching Thee by that exceeding pain, and by the crushing burden of Thy heavy Cross to be merciful to me, a sinner, to forgive me all my mortal and venial sins, and to lead me on towards Heaven along the Way of Thy Cross. Amen.

Imprimatur: Thomas D. Beven, Bishop of Springfield.

It is related in the annals of Clairvaux that St. Bernard asked our Lord which was His greatest unrecorded suffering, and Our Lord answered: *"I had on My Shoulder, while I bore My Cross on the Way of Sorrows, a grievous Wound, which was more painful than the others, and which is not recorded by men. Honor this wound with thy devotion, and I will grant thee whatsoever thou dost ask through its virtue and merit. And in regard to all those who shall venerate this Wound, I will remit to them all their venial sins, and will no longer remember their mortal sins."*

OUR BLESSED MOTHER

All of us at one time or another have the sense that we could use some help when approaching God. Let's contemplate the profound love Mary has for her Son. She was with Him from His birth, during His ministry, and stood at the foot of The Cross when Jesus died. Now let's reflect on the overwhelming love that Jesus has for His mother. Recall the sorrow that pieced Mary's heart when she witnessed Jesus at the point of exhaustion, carrying His cross, carrying it to His Crucifixion…how many tears were shed at that moment? Words fail to fully capture the tremendous love Jesus and His mother have for each other.

Mary's finest hour was her *fiat*, her complete surrender to God. She responded to the Archangel Gabriel, who announced to her that she would bear the Christ child: *"Behold, I am the handmaid of the Lord. May it be done to me according to your word." Then the angel departed from her."* **Luke 1:38** All of heaven must have rejoiced at Mary's yes! She could have said no, but through her faithfulness, obedience, and love of God she completely and freely gave herself to God almighty. Mary's *fiat* resounds still today, through all of eternity, and all of heaven; she glorifies God in a distinctive and uniquely eternal way. The **Memorare** is a beautiful prayer to remind us we have a wonderful friend, an advocate and defender, Mary the mother of our Lord. Her last words recorded in the Gospel *"Do what ever He tells you."* **John. 2:5**. Referring to her Son as she addressed the servers during the wedding of Cana.

The Blessed Virgin Mary will always lead you to her Son. In our prayers to her, we glorify and worship her Son; we reflect on the life of Christ, and on salvation history. Jesus is more than happy to receive His mother's request and prayers on our behalf. Remember that the first miracle by Christ which revealed His glory and launched His public ministry was the wedding miracle of Cana; Mary is the one who turned to her Son Jesus and said, *"They have no wine."* The Son did not ignore His mother's request. During our daily lives we ask our friends or family members to pray for us, and the Lord certainly hears those prayers. How much more so when those prayers are offered by saints in the presence of The Holy Trinity! They prayed for us while on earth…why would they stop once in heaven? † *MSG Michael Cutone*

MEMORARE

"Remember, O most gracious Virgin Mary, that never was it known that anyone who fled to your protection, implored your help, or sought your intercession, was left unaided. Inspired with this confidence, I fly to you, O virgin of virgins, my mother. To you I come, before you I stand, sinful and sorrowful. O mother of the Word Incarnate! Despise not my petitions, but in your mercy hear and answer me. Amen." **St. Bernard of Clairvaux**

St. Bernard of Clairvaux composed the famous prayer to the Most Blessed Virgin Mary known as *The Memorare*

THE CHURCH AND THE SAINTS REGARDING MARY

St. Louis De Montfort on praying to Mary *"By asking Mary to approach Him for us we are practicing humility, something which always gladdens the heart of God!" St. Francis de Sales reminds us "God so loves humility that He instantly hastens to the soul in which he sees it."*

"This motherhood of Mary in the order of grace continues uninterruptedly from the consent which she loyally gave at the Annunciation and which she sustained without wavering beneath the cross, until the eternal fulfillment of all the elect. Taken up to heaven she did not lay aside this saving office but by her manifold intercession continues to bring us the gifts of eternal salvation. By her maternal charity, she cares for the brethren of her Son, who still journey on earth surrounded by dangers and difficulties, until they are led into their blessed home. Therefore the Blessed Virgin is invoked in the Church under the titles of Advocate, Helper, Benefactress, and Mediatrix. This, however, is so understood that it neither takes away anything from nor adds anything to the dignity and efficacy of Christ the one Mediator."

(*Lumen Gentium* Vatican II §62.)

SAINT CYRIL OF JERUSALEM DOCTOR OF THE CHURCH

Saint Cyril: Mary's role in relation to the teaching of the Church. *"He was made man, not in appearance only or as a phantasm, but in a real way. He did not pass through the Virgin, as through a channel; rather He truly took flesh from her and by her was truly nursed, really eating and really drinking just as we do. For if the Incarnation were a mere appearance, such would be our redemption as well. In Christ there were two aspects: man, who was visible in Him, and God, who remained invisible...."* **Luigi Gambero, S.M.,** Mary and the Fathers of the Church pg 133.
Catecheses 4,9; PG 33, 465 B-468 A

MAGNIFICAT

"My soul doth magnify the Lord: And my spirit hath rejoiced in God my **Saviour**. Because He hath regarded the lowliness of His handmaid. For, behold, from henceforth all generations shall call me blessed. For He that is mighty, hath done great things to me, and holy is His Name. And his mercy is from generation unto generations, to them that fear Him. He hath showed might with His arm. He hath scattered the proud in the conceit of their heart. He hath put down the mighty from their seat, and hath exalted the lowly. He hath filled the hungry with good things; and the rich he hath sent away empty. He hath received Israel His servant, being mindful of His mercy. As He spoke to our fathers, to Abraham and to his seed forever." **(Luke 1: 41-45)**

2617. Mary's prayer is revealed to us at the dawning of the fullness of time. Before the incarnation of the Son of God, and before the outpouring of the Holy Spirit, her prayer cooperates in a unique way with the Father's plan of loving kindness: at the Annunciation, for Christ's conception; at Pentecost, for the formation of the Church, his Body.[88]

In the faith of his humble handmaid, the Gift of God found the acceptance he had awaited from the beginning of time. She whom the Almighty made "full of grace" responds by offering her whole being: "Behold I am the handmaid of the Lord; let it be [done] to me according to your word." "*Fiat*": this is Christian prayer: to be wholly God's, because he is wholly ours.

2618. The Gospel reveals to us how Mary prays and intercedes in faith. At Cana,[89] the mother of Jesus asks her son for the needs of a wedding feast; this is the sign of another feast - that of the wedding of the Lamb where he gives his body and blood at the request of the Church, his Bride. It is at the hour of the New Covenant, at the foot of the cross,[90] that Mary is heard as the Woman, the new Eve, the true "Mother of all the living."

88 Cf.*Lk*1:38; Acts 1:14.
89 Cf.*Jn* 2:1-12.
90 Cf.*Jn* 19:25-27

2674. Mary gave her consent in faith at the Annunciation and maintained it without hesitation at the foot of the Cross. Ever since, her motherhood has extended to the brothers and sisters of her Son "who still journey on earth surrounded by dangers and difficulties."[28]

28 *LG* 62.

Catechism of the Catholic Church. Libreria Editrice Vaticana ©1997

SIC DEVS DILEXIT MVNDVM

Consecration to Jesus Christ, the Incarnate Wisdom, through the Blessed Virgin Mary by St. Louis De Montfort

"O Eternal and Incarnate Wisdom! O sweetest and most adorable Jesus! True God and true man, only Son of the Eternal Father, and of Mary, always virgin! I adore Thee profoundly in the bosom and splendors of Thy Father during eternity; and I adore Thee also in the virginal bosom of Mary, Thy most worthy Mother, in the time of Thine Incarnation. I give Thee thanks for that Thou hast annihilated Thyself, taking the form of a slave in order to rescue me from the cruel slavery of the devil. I praise and glorify Thee for that Thou hast been pleased to submit Thyself to Mary, Thy holy Mother, in all things, in order to make me Thy faithful slave through her. But, alas! Ungrateful and faithless as I have been, I have not kept the promises which I made so solemnly to Thee in my Baptism; I have not fulfilled my obligations; I do not deserve to be called Thy child, nor yet Thy slave; and as there is nothing in me which does not merit Thine anger and Thy repulse, I dare not come by myself before Thy most holy and august Majesty.

It is on this account that I have recourse to the intercession of Thy most holy Mother, whom Thou hast given me for a mediatrix with Thee. It is through her that I hope to obtain of Thee contrition, the pardon of my sins, and the acquisition and preservation of wisdom.

Hail, then, O Immaculate Mary, living tabernacle of the Divinity, where the Eternal Wisdom willed to be hidden and to be adored by angels and by men! Hail, O Queen of Heaven and earth, to whose empire everything is subject which is under God. Hail, O sure refuge of sinners, whose mercy fails no one. Hear the desires which I have of the Divine Wisdom; and for that end receive the vows and offerings which in my lowliness I present to thee.

I, (Name), a faithless sinner, renew and ratify today in thy hands the vows of my Baptism; I renounce forever Satan, his pomps and works; and I give myself entirely to Jesus Christ, the Incarnate Wisdom, to carry my cross after Him all the days of my life, and to be more faithful to Him than I have ever been before.
In the presence of all the heavenly court I choose thee this day for my Mother and Mistress. I deliver and consecrate to thee, as thy slave, my body and soul, my goods, both interior and exterior, and even the value of all my good actions, past, present and future; leaving to thee the entire and full right of disposing of me, and all that belongs to me, without exception, according to thy good pleasure, for the greater glory of God, in time and in eternity.
Receive, O benignant Virgin, this little offering of my slavery, in honor of, and in union with, that subjection which the Eternal Wisdom deigned to have to thy maternity, in homage to the power which both of you have over this poor sinner, and in thanksgiving for the privileges with which the Holy Trinity has

favored thee. I declare that I wish henceforth, as thy true slave, to seek thy honor and to obey thee in all things.

O admirable Mother, present me to thy dear Son as His eternal slave, so that as He has redeemed me by thee, by thee He may receive me! O Mother of mercy, grant me the grace to obtain the true Wisdom of God; and for that end receive me among those whom thou lovest and teachest, whom thou leadest, nourishest and protectest as thy children and thy slaves.

O faithful Virgin, make me in all things so perfect a disciple, imitator and slave of the Incarnate Wisdom, Jesus Christ thy Son, that I may attain, by thine intercession and by thine example, to the fullness of His age on earth and of His glory in Heaven. Amen."

St. Louis De Montfort True Devotion To Mary

Photograph taken by MSG Michael Cutone

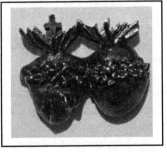

AN OFFERING OF THE HEARTS OF JESUS AND MARY

"O Jesus, only Son of God, only Son of Mary, I offer Thee the most loving Heart of Thy divine Mother which is more precious and pleasing to Thee than all hearts. O Mary, Mother of Jesus, I offer Thee the most adorable Heart of Thy well-beloved Son, who is the life and love and joy of Thy Heart. Blessed be the Most Loving Heart and Sweet Name of Our Lord Jesus Christ and the most glorious Virgin Mary, His Mother, in eternity and forever. Amen."

St. John Eudes

ACT OF CONSECRATION TO THE SACRED HEART

For God so loved the world... **John 3:16**

"O Sacred Heart of Jesus, to Thee I consecrate and offer up my person and my life, my actions, trials, and sufferings, that my entire being may henceforth only be employed in loving, honoring and glorifying Thee. This is my irrevocable will, to belong entirely to Thee, and to do all for Thy love, renouncing with my whole heart all that can displease Thee. I take Thee, O Sacred Heart, for the sole object of my love, the protection of my life, the pledge of my salvation, the remedy of my frailty and inconstancy, the reparation for all the defects of my life, and my secure refuge at the hour of my death. Be Thou, O Most Merciful Heart, my justification before God Thy Father, and screen me from His anger which I have so justly merited. I fear all from my own weakness and malice, but placing my entire confidence in Thee, O Heart of Love, I hope all from Thine infinite Goodness. Annihilate in me all that can displease or resist Thee. Imprint Thy pure love so deeply in my heart that I may never forget Thee or be separated from Thee. I beseech Thee, through Thine infinite Goodness, grant that my name be engraved upon Thy Heart, for in this I place all my happiness and all my glory, to live and to die as one of Thy devoted servants. Amen."

St. Margaret Mary Alacoque

SIC DEVS DILEXIT MVNDVM

CONSECRATION OF THE HUMAN RACE TO THE SACRED HEART OF JESUS

Most sweet Jesus, Redeemer of the human race, look down upon us humbly prostrate before Thine altar. We are Thine, and Thine we wish to be; but, to be more surely united with Thee, behold each one of us freely consecrates himself today to Thy most Sacred Heart.

Many indeed have never known Thee; many too, despising Thy precepts, have rejected Thee. Have mercy on them all, most merciful Jesus, and draw them to Thy sacred Heart. Be Thou King, O Lord, not only of the faithful who have never forsaken Thee, but also of the prodigal children who have abandoned Thee; grant that they may quickly return to Thy Father's house lest they die of wretchedness and hunger.

Be Thou King of those who are deceived by erroneous opinions, or whom discord keeps aloof, and call them back to the harbor of truth and unity of faith, so that there may be but one flock and one Shepherd.

Be Thou King of all those who are still involved in the darkness of idolatry or of Islamism, and refuse not to draw them into the light and kingdom of God. Turn Thine eyes of mercy towards the children of the race, once Thy chosen people: of old they called down upon themselves the Blood of the Savior; may it now descend upon them a laver of redemption and of life.
Grant, O Lord, to Thy Church assurance of freedom and immunity from harm; give peace and order to all nations, and make the earth resound from pole to pole with one cry: "Praise be to the divine Heart that wrought our salvation; to it be glory and honor for ever. Amen.

SIC DEVS DILEXIT MVNDVM

WHAT THE CATECHISM OF THE CATHOLIC CHURCH HAS TO SAY ABOUT THE EUCHARIST

1323 "At the Last Supper, on the night he was betrayed, our Savior instituted the Eucharistic sacrifice of his Body and Blood. This he did in order to perpetuate the sacrifice of the cross throughout the ages until he should come again, and so to entrust to his beloved Spouse, the Church, a memorial of his death and resurrection: a sacrament of love, a sign of unity, a bond of charity, a Paschal banquet 'in which Christ is consumed, the mind is filled with grace, and a pledge of future glory is given to us."[135]

THE EUCHARIST - SOURCE AND SUMMIT OF THE CHURCH

1324 The Eucharist is "the source and summit of the Christian life."[136] "The other sacraments, and indeed all ecclesiastical ministries and works of the apostolate, are bound up with the Eucharist and are oriented toward it. For in the blessed Eucharist is contained the whole spiritual good of the Church, namely Christ himself, our Pasch."[137]

135 SC 47.
136 *LG* 11.
137 *PO* 5.

Catechism of the Catholic Church. Libreria Editrice Vaticana ©1997

WHAT THE SAINTS HAVE SAID ABOUT THE HOLY MASS

"When we receive Holy Communion, we experience something extraordinary - a joy, a fragrance, a well being that thrills the whole body and causes it to exalt." "If we really understood the Mass, we would die of joy." "There is nothing so great as the Eucharist. If God had something more precious, He would have given it to us." "When we have been to Holy Communion, the balm of love envelops the soul as the flower envelops the bee."
St. John Vianney Patron Saint of Parish Priests

For each Mass we hear with devotion, Our Lord sends a saint to comfort us at death.
Revelation of Christ to St. Gertrude the Great

He who is in the habit of devoutly hearing holy Mass shall in death be consoled by the presence of the angels and saints, his advocates, who shall bravely defend him from all the snares of infernal spirits.
Revelation of Christ to St. Mechtilde

"The Mass is the most perfect form of prayer!" **Pope Paul VI**

"The Holy Mass would be of greater profit if people had it offered in their lifetime, rather than having it celebrated for the relief of their souls after death."
Pope Benedict XV

"The celebration of Holy Mass is as valuable as the death of Jesus on the cross." **St. Thomas Aquinas**

"The heavens open and multitudes of angels come to assist in the Holy Sacrifice of the Mass."

"It is most true that he who attends holy Mass shall be freed from many evils and from many dangers, both seen and unseen."
St. Gregory

"The angels surround and help the priest when he is celebrating Mass." *He who devoutly hears holy Mass will receive a great vigor to enable him to resist mortal sin, and there shall be pardoned to him all venial sins which he may have committed up to that hour.""He [who attends Mass with all possible devotion] shall be freed from sudden death, which is the most terrible stroke launched by the Divine Justice against sinners. Behold a wonderful preservative against sudden death."*
St. Augustine

"Without doubt, the Lord grants all favors which are asked of Him in Mass, provided they be fitting for us; and, which is a matter of great wonder, ofttimes He also grants that also which is not demanded of Him, if we, on our part, put no obstacle in the way."
St. Jerome

"When Mass is being celebrated, the sanctuary is filled with countless angels who adore the divine victim immolated on the altar." **St. John Chrysostom**

"A single Mass offered for oneself during life may be worth more than a thousand celebrated for the same intention after death."
St. Anselm

Once, St. Teresa was overwhelmed with God's Goodness and asked Our Lord "How can I thank you?" Our Lord replied, "ATTEND ONE MASS." St. Teresa

SIC DEVS DILEXIT MVNDVM

"One single Mass gives more honor to God than all the penances of the Saints, the labors of the Apostles, the sufferings of the Martyrs and even the burning love of the Blessed Mother of God."
St. Alphonsus Liguori

"Man should tremble, the world should vibrate, all Heaven should be deeply moved when the Son of God appears on the altar in the hands of the priest." **St. Francis of Assisi**

"Oh, if we could only understand Who is that God Whom we receive in Holy Communion, then what purity of heart we would bring to Him!" **St. Mary Magdalen of Pazzi**

"The offering up of the Holy Mass benefits not only the saints for whom [in whose honor] it is said, but the whole Church of God in Heaven, on earth and in Purgatory." **St. John Vianney**

"When we go before the Blessed Sacrament, let us open our heart; our good God will open His. We shall go to Him; He will come to us; the one to ask, the other to receive. It will be like a breath from one to the other." **St. John Vianney**

"It would be easier for the earth to carry on without the sun than without the Holy Mass." **St. Padre Pio, Stigmatic Priest**

"All my sermons are prepared in the presence of the Blessed Sacrament. As recreation is most pleasant and profitable in the sun, so homiletic creativity is best nourished before the Eucharist. The most brilliant ideas come from meeting God face to face. The Holy Spirit that presided at the Incarnation is the best atmosphere for illumination. Pope John Paul II keeps a small desk or writing pad near him whenever he is in the presence of the Blessed Sacrament; and I have done this all my life —I am sure for the same reason he does, because a lover always works better when the beloved is with him." **Archbishop Fulton J. Sheen**

"The Lord Jesus himself proclaims, 'This is My Body.' Before the blessing of the heavenly words something of another character is spoken of; [bread]. After consecration it is designated 'body'. He himself speaks of his blood. Before the consecration it is spoken of as something else; [wine]. After the consecration it is spoken of as 'blood'. And you say, 'Amen' ~ that is, 'It is true.' What the mouth speaks, let the mind within confess; what the tongue utters, let the heart feel." **St. Ambrose, Bishop of Milan**

"If the Angels could envy, they would envy us for Holy Communion." **St. Pope Pius X**

"The celebration of the Holy Mass is as valuable as the death of Jesus on the Cross." **St. Thomas Aquinas**

"You envy the opportunity of the woman who touched the vestments of Jesus, of the sinful woman who washed His feet with her tears, of the women of Galilee who had the happiness of following Him in His pilgrimages, of the Apostles and disciples who conversed with Him familiarly, of the people of the time who listened to the words of grace and salvation which came forth from His lips. You call happy those who saw Him...But, come to the altar and you will see Him, you will touch Him, you will give to Him holy kisses, you will wash Him with your tears, you will carry Him within you like Mary Most Holy." **St. John Chrysostom Doctor of The Church**

SIC DEVS DILEXIT MVNDVM

PRAYER TO OBTAIN THE GRACE OF ALL THE WORLD'S MASSES

Eternal Father, we humbly offer Thee our poor presence, and that of the whole of humanity, from the beginning to the end of the world at all the Masses that ever have or ever will be prayed. We offer Thee all the pains, sufferings, prayers, sacrifices, joys, and relaxations of our lives, in union with those of our Lord Jesus. here on earth. May the Most Precious Blood of Christ, all His Blood, Wounds, and Agony save us, through the Sorrowful and Immaculate Heart of Mary. Amen.

WHY WE SHOULD ATTEND MASS

Christ is substantially present (body, blood, soul and divinity) during Mass. For any Christian, you would think this incredible gift and knowledge alone would bring millions to Mass everyday! Sadly, most Catholics fail to understand that true God is substantially present during the Holy Mass. The Sacrifice of Calvary is present, along with a multitude of angels praising Christ. Yet in today's world, we often turn our backs on the Lord. We often fail to take even one day a week to properly honor His Sacrifice that He endured on the Cross for the salvation of man!

We have taken God out of our schools, work, government, and our lives; many of us will not spend one hour with our Savior.

We have abandoned God, and we ask why there is suffering, war, sickness, and all types of horrors. Our Merciful Savior has not abandoned us. He is truly present at each and every Mass around the world! We have abandoned God.

If we understood the true wonders of the Mass, not only we would attend Mass on Sundays, but every day. Each and every Mass around the world would be filled with souls. Attending and participating in the Mass is the best way to obtain infinite graces, mercies, and blessings from God. A single Mass far outweighs all the virtues and deeds in the history of humankind. Nothing in the world is more precious and wonderful then the Holy Mass. This is the profound love Jesus has for all of mankind, the Creator of the Universe allowed His only Son, to be tortured and crucified by His creatures "so that we might be reconciled to God by the death of his Son".

Our country is fighting a global war or terrorism. Radical Islamic terrorist are committed to the destruction of Western Civilization and America; the US economy is in serious peril and some economist would argue on the brink of collapse. The United States alone has aborted 48 million babies since the passing of _Roe v Wade,_ innocent infants are killed in their mother's womb every day. If there is ever a time to attend Mass, it is now!

† MSG Michael Cutone

"The Mass is the greatest wonder in the world. There is nothing on earth equal to it, and there is nothing in Heaven greater than it."

Fr. Paul O'Sullivan, O.P.

IS THE HOLY MASS ONE AND THE SAME SACRIFICE WITH THAT OF THE CROSS? "The Holy Mass is one and the same Sacrifice with that of the Cross, inasmuch as Christ, who offered Himself, a bleeding victim, on the cross to His Heavenly Father, continues to offer Himself in an unbloody manner on the altar, through the ministry of His priests"

FOR WHAT ENDS IS THE SACRIFICE OF THE MASS OFFERED? The Sacrifice of the Mass is offered for four ends: first, to give supreme honor and glory to God; second, to thank Him for all His benefits; third, to satisfy God for our sins and to obtain grace of repentance; and fourth to obtain all other graces and blessings through Jesus Christ." Cannon Francis Ripley. **This is The Faith.**

The Wonders of the Mass. By Fr. Paul O'Sullivan O.P. "A remarkable and inspiring book that educates Christian readers to the true meaning, wonder and power of the Holy Mass. Every Catholic should read and own this book". *✝ MSG Michael M. Cutone*

Excerpts from: **The Wonders of the Mass**, Fr. Paul O'Sullivan, O.P.

"The saints never speak so eloquently as when they speak of the Mass. They can never say enough on this sublime subject, for St. Bonaventure says that the wonders of the Mass are as many as there are stars in the heavens and grains of sand on the seashores of the world. The graces, blessings, and favors granted to those who assist at this Divine Sacrifice are beyond all comprehension.

SIC DEVS DILEXIT MVNDVM

The Mass is the greatest wonder in the world. There is nothing on earth equal to it, and there is nothing in Heaven greater than it. The next greatest wonder is the indifference and ignorance of Catholics regarding Holy Mass. How is it that so many Catholics do not go to Mass?

The great Sacrifice of Calvary is offered near their homes, almost at their very doors, and they are too slothful to assist at it. The Sacrifice of Calvary? Yes, for the Mass is really and truly the very same as the Death of Jesus on the Cross.

What is the Mass?

1. **In the Mass, the Son of God becomes man again**, so that in every Mass the stupendous Mystery of the Incarnation, with all its infinite merits, is repeated as truly as when the Son of God first took flesh in the womb of the Virgin Mary.

St. Augustine: "What a sublime dignity is that of the priest, in whose hands Christ once more becomes man!"

2. **The Mass is the birth of Jesus Christ.** He is really born on the altar each time that Mass is said, as He was born in Bethlehem.

St. John Damascene: "If anyone wishes to know how the bread is changed into the Body of Jesus Christ, I will tell him. The Holy Ghost over-shadows the priest, and acts on him as He acted on the Blessed Virgin Mary."

St. Bonaventure: "God, when He descends upon the altar, does no less than He did when He became man the first time in the womb of the Virgin Mary."

3. **The Mass is the same as the sacrifice of Calvary.** In it, God dies as He died on the first Good Friday. It has the same infinite value of Calvary, and brings down on men the same priceless graces. The Mass is not an imitation nor a memory of Calvary; it is identically the same sacrifice, and differs only from

Calvary in appearance. In every Mass, the Blood of Jesus is shed for us again.

St. Augustine: "In the Mass, the Blood of Christ flows anew for sinners."

4. **Nothing on this earth**, nothing in Heaven itself gives more glory to God and obtains more benefits for us than a single Mass.

5. **By the Mass, we offer to God** the greatest praise, the greatest glory He could possibly desire. We give Him most perfect thanks for all the benefits He has bestowed on us. We make more reparation for our faults than by the severest penances.

6. **We can do nothing better** for the conversion of sinners than offer for them the Holy Sacrifice of the Mass. If mothers would only hear and get Masses said for their erring children, and wives for their husbands, how happy their families would be!

7. **No prayers, no suffrages**, no matter how fervent, can help the Holy Souls as the Mass. Oh, let us think of the Souls in Purgatory. Among them may be our dear father and mother and friends. We can help them most easily, we can relieve their awful pains most efficaciously, by hearing Mass for them.

The benefits of the Mass

St. Thomas, the prince of theologians, write wonderfully of the Mass. **"The Mass,"** he says, *"obtains for sinners in mortal sin the grace of repentance. For the just, it obtains the remission of venial sins and the pardon of the pain due to sin. It obtains an increase of habitual (sanctifying) grace, as well as all the graces necessary for their special needs."*

Our Lord said to St. Mechtilde: "In Mass I come with such humility that there is no sinner, no matter how depraved he be, that I am not ready to receive, if only he desires it. I come with such sweetness and mercy that I will pardon my greatest enemies, if they ask for pardon. I come with such generosity that there is no one so poor that I will not fill him with the riches of my love. I come with such heavenly food as will strengthen the weakest, with such light as will illumine the blindest, with such a plenitude of graces as will remove all miseries, overcome all obstinacy, and dissipate all fears."

What words of divine comfort — words of God Himself. If we heard nothing else about the Holy Sacrifice of the Mass, are not these words alone sufficient to fill us with faith and confidence in the Divine Mysteries.

At the Sanctus, we should remember that the Angels come down to assist at Mass in multitudes, and that we are in the midst of them, and we should join our voices with theirs in adoring and praising God. They present our prayers to God.

At the Consecration, we should be filled with the deepest reverence and love, for Jesus is really born in the hands of the priest, as He was born in Bethlehem. When the priest lifts up the Sacred Host, we should look on our God in an ecstasy of joy, as the Angels look on Him in Heaven, and say, "My Lord and my God."

At the Consecration of the Precious Blood, we must remember that all the Precious Blood that Jesus shed on Calvary is in the chalice, and we should offer it to God with the priest for God's glory and for our own intentions. It is well to place ourselves, our sins, all our intentions, our dear ones, the souls in Purgatory in all the chalices being ,at this moment, offered to God in every part of the world.

We must be full of holy awe and love from the Consecration to the Communion. We are in the midst of countless adoring Angels. Remember: the day you hear Mass is worth a thousand days to you, that all the labors and work of a day, or a week, or a whole year, are nothing in comparison with the value of one Mass."

By Fr. Paul O'Sullvian, O.P.

THE CATHOLIC CHURCH

"The Church, instituted by the Lord and confirmed by the Apostles, is one for all men; but the frantic folly of the diverse impious acts sects has cut them off from her. It cannot be denied that this tearing asunder of the faith has arisen from the defect of poor intelligence, which twists what is read to conform to its opinion, instead of adjusting its opinion to the meaning of what is read. However, while individual parties fight among themselves, the Church stands revealed not only by her own doctrines, but by those also of her adversaries. And although they are all arranged against her, she confutes the most wicked error which they all share, by the very fact that she is alone and One. All the heretics, therefore, come against the Church; but while all the heretics can conquer each other, they can win nothing for themselves. For their victory is the triumph of the Church over all of them. One heresy struggles against that teaching of another, which the faith of the Church has already condemned in the other heresy, - for there is nothing which the heretics hold in common, ' and the result is that they affirm our faith while fighting among themselves."

   St. Hilary of Poitiers - The Trinity, 7:4, 356 A.D.. Jurgens 865

ST. CYRIL DOCTOR OF THE CHURCH ON THE EUCHARIST

"The doctrine of the real Presence is clearly affirmed by St. Cyril: "Since He Himself has declared and said of the bread: *"This is My Body,"* who shall dare to doubt any more? And When He asserts and says: *"This is My Blood."* Who shall ever hesitate and say it is not His Blood?"

St. Cyril writes: Do not think it mere bread and wine, for it is the Body and Blood of Christ, according to the Lord's declaration. [Moreover,] Having learned this and being assured of it, that what appears to be bread is not bread, though [so] perceived by the taste, but the Body of Christ, and what appears to be wine is not wine, through the taste says so, but the Blood of Christ…strengthen thy heart, partaking of it as spiritual [food], and rejoice the face of thy soul." **Fr. Christopher Rengers, O.F.M**. The 33 Doctors of the Church..

"What is the Sacrament of the Holy Eucharist? The Sacrament of the Holy Eucharist is true Body and Blood of Jesus Christ, together with His Soul and Divinity, under the appearance of bread and wine." **Canon Francis Ripley,** This Is The Faith

THE BREAD OF LIFE DISCOURSE: GOSPEL OF JOHN

In the Gospel of John, Christ refers to himself as "the bread of life." From **John 6:33 to 6:58** there are seven verses that refer to "the bread of life," such as "who ever eats this bread shall have eternal life." Who is the bread of life? Jesus. He declares it…who shall say it is not so? Jesus said to them *"I am the bread of life; whoever comes to me will never hunger, and whoever believes in me will never thirst.'* **John 6:35**

SIC DEVS DILEXIT MVNDVM

To understand why this is significant, let's begin with the birth of Jesus. Reflect on this profound event, the single event that changed the history of the world. The creator of the universe came as an infant, an innocent child, so man could approach him with humble trust. The Word becomes flesh and dwells among us. When we consider in contemplative prayer the gift of Christ' birth, how can we fail to appreciate its significance? Likewise, we must understand the significance of Bethlehem and the manger. Bethlehem in Hebrew translates to *"The House of Bread."* Jesus is placed in a manger. Why is this important? The birth description of Jesus is also foreshadowing of Holy Communion, the Eucharist.
"I am the living bread that came down from heaven; whoever eats this bread will live forever; and the bread that I will give is my flesh for the life of the world." **John 6:54**. A manger is used to feed farm animals. Jesus is referred to as "the bread of life" in scripture. It is us who will feed from "the manger" eating the bread of life, Jesus. He nourishes our soul, and gives us eternal life

Another crucial verse to consider during "The Bread of Life Discourse" between Jesus and the disciples is John 6:66 ***"As a result of this, many (of) his disciples returned to their former way of life and no longer accompanied him."*** The disciples found this teaching too hard. Note the scripture verse number. Now notice the action of the disciples; *"they left Jesus and returned to the former way of life."* They could not believe that eating the Body of Jesus, and drinking His Blood would give them eternal life. This heresy still exists; times have not changed…today, we have many Catholics and other Christians who refuse to believe that The Holy Eucharist is the real presence of Christ: Body, Blood, Soul and Divinity. How much sorrow must be afflicted upon Our Lord?

† MSG Michael Cutone

Gospel of John 6:48-68 (NAB)

"48 I am the bread of life. 49Your ancestors ate the manna in the desert, but they died; 50 this is the bread that comes down from heaven so that one may eat it and not die. 51 I am the living bread that came down from heaven; whoever eats this bread will live forever; and the bread that I will give is my flesh for the life of the world." 52 The Jews quarreled among themselves, saying, "How can this man give us (his) flesh to eat?" 53 Jesus said to them, "Amen, amen, I say to you, unless you eat the flesh of the Son of Man and drink his blood, you do not have life within you. 54 Whoever eats my flesh and drinks my blood has eternal life, and I will raise him on the last day. 55 For my flesh is true food, and my blood is true drink. 56 Whoever eats my flesh and drinks my blood remains in me and I in him. 57 Just as the living Father sent me and I have life because of the Father, so also the one who feeds on me will have life because of me. 58 This is the bread that came down from heaven. Unlike your ancestors who ate and still died, whoever eats this bread will live forever."

59 These things he said while teaching in the synagogue in Capernaum. 60 Then many of his disciples who were listening said, "This saying is hard; who can accept it?" 61 Since Jesus knew that his disciples were murmuring about this, he said to them, "Does this shock you? 62 What if you were to see the Son of Man ascending to where he was before? 63 It is the spirit that gives life, while the flesh is of no avail. The words I have spoken to you are spirit and life. 64 But there are some of you who do not believe." Jesus knew from the beginning the ones who would not believe and the one who would betray him. 65 And he said, "For this reason I have told you that no one can come to me unless it is granted him by my Father." **66 As a result of this, many (of) his disciples returned to their former way of life and no longer accompanied him.** 67 Jesus then said to the Twelve, "Do you also want to leave?" 68 Simon Peter answered him, "Master, to whom shall we go? You have the words of eternal life." **John 6:48-68**

SIC DEVS DILEXIT MVNDVM

THE AGONY OF THE GARDEN

Christ took along with Him, Peter, James, and John. Jesus stated to them *"My soul is sorrowful even to death. Remain here and keep watch."* Listen carefully to His words; *"Remain here and keep watch."* Jesus *"advanced a little and fell to the ground and prayed that if it were possible the hour might pass by him; he said, "Abba, Father, all things are possible to you. Take this cup away from me, but not what I will but what you will."*

"When he returned he found them asleep. He said to Peter, "Simon, are you asleep? Could you not keep watch for one hour?" Watch and pray that you may not undergo the test. The spirit is willing but the flesh is weak." Withdrawing again, he prayed, saying the same thing. Then he returned once more and found them asleep, for they could not keep their eyes open and did not know what to answer him. He returned a third time and said to them, "Are you still sleeping and taking your rest? It is enough. The hour has come. Behold, the Son of Man is to be handed over to sinners. Get up, let us go. See, my betrayer is at hand." **Mark 14:34-42.**

Three times, the Apostles fell asleep. Three times, the Lord had to wake them up. How many times have we fallen asleep on the Lord? How many times have we been asleep when we should have been on watch, staying up with the Lord? Christ tells his astonished

Apostles *"Behold, the Son of Man is to be handed over to sinners."* The very next line is a command to the Apostles; Jesus says *"Get up, let us go. See, my betrayer is at hand."* Who among us will follow the Lord's command? Who among us will pick up their cross, and follow Christ. The world is asleep *"Get up, let us go. See, my betrayer is at hand."* Christ is calling each and every one of us! Pick up your cross and draw fire. *† MSG Michael Cutone*

CHAPLET OF DIVINE MERCY

During 1931 incredible events unfolded with Sister Maria Faustina; a nun with the Congregation of the Sisters of Our Lady of Mercy located in Poland. She would have numerous visions and encounters with Christ. He spoke to her about His unfathomable Mercy for sinners. Christ presented to Sister Faustina a prayer called the Chaplet of Divine Mercy, and His desire to have this prayer taught throughout the world. Jesus instructed Sister Faustina to have an image of Him painted with the words *"Jesus, I trust in You"* below the image. Sister Faustina herself provided the details of the image she witnessed. For information on the incredible story of the Chaplet of the Divine Mercy and Saint Faustina visit: http://thedivinemercy.org/message/

SIC DEVS DILEXIT MVNDVM

FROM ST. FAUSTINA'S DIARY

"O Blood and Water, which gushed forth from the Heart of Jesus as a fount of mercy for us, I trust in You!" (Diary 84). "Encourage souls to say the Chaplet which I have given you (Diary 1541) . . . Whoever will recite it will receive great mercy at the hour of death (Diary 687) . . . When they say this Chaplet in the presence of the dying, I will stand between My Father and the dying person, not as the Judge but as the Merciful Saviour (Diary 1541) . . . Priests will recommend it to sinners as their last hope of salvation. Even if there were a sinner most hardened, if he were to recite this Chaplet only once, he would receive grace from My infinite Mercy (Diary 687) . . . I desire to grant unimaginable graces to those souls who trust in My Mercy (Diary 687) . . . Through the Chaplet you will obtain everything, if what you ask for is compatible with My will." (Diary 1731)

HOW TO RECITE THE CHAPLET OF DIVINE MERCY

The Chaplet of Mercy is recited using ordinary rosary beads of five decades. **Begin with the Our Father, the Hail Mary and the Apostle's Creed:**

Then, on the large bead before each decade:
Eternal Father, I offer you the Body and Blood, Soul and Divinity, of Your Dearly Beloved Son, Our Lord, Jesus Christ, in atonement for our sins and those of the whole world.

On the ten small beads of each decade, say: **For the sake of His sorrowful Passion, have mercy on us, and on the whole world.**

Conclude with (Say Three Times):
Holy God,
Holy Mighty One,
Holy Immortal One,
have mercy on us
and on the whole world.

PRAYERS FOR OUR POPE: O God, the Shepherd and Ruler of all Your faithful people, mercifully look upon Your servant [name of Pope], whom You have chosen as the chief Shepherd to preside over Your Church. We beg You to help him edify, both by word and example, those over whom he has charge, that he may reach everlasting life together with the flock entrusted to him. Through Christ our Lord. Amen. **Lord, source of eternal life and truth, give to Your shepherd, the Pope, a spirit of courage and right judgment, a spirit of knowledge and love.** By governing with fidelity those entrusted to his care may he, as successor to the apostle Peter and vicar of Christ, build Your church into a sacrament of unity, love, and peace for all the world. We ask this through our Lord Jesus Christ, Your Son, Who lives and reigns with You and the Holy
Spirit, one God, forever and ever. Amen

A PRAYER FOR PRIESTS
By *the late John J Cardinal Carberry*

Keep them; I pray Thee, dearest Lord. Keep them, for they are Thine- The priests whose lives burn out before Thy consecrated shrine. Keep them, for they are in the world, Though from the world apart. When earthly pleasures tempt, allure --Shelter them in Thy heart. Keep them and comfort them in hours Of loneliness and pain, When all their life of sacrifice For souls seems but in vain. Keep them and remember, Lord, they have no one but Thee. Yet, they have only human hearts, With human frailty. Keep them as spotless as the Host, that daily they caress; Their every thought and word and deed, Deign, dearest Lord, to bless. Amen.

SIC DEVS DILEXIT MVNDVM

Our Father, Hail Mary. Mary Queen of the Clergy, Pray for them.

THE FIFTEEN PRAYERS REVEALED BY OUR LORD TO SAINT BRIDGET OF SWEDEN

St. Bridget prayed fervently in front of the Tabernacle wishing to know for some time, the number of blows Our Lord suffered during His Passion. Jesus honored her request one day by appearing to her and told her, *"I received 5480 blows on My Body. If you wish to honor them in some way, say 15 Our Fathers and 15 Hail Marys with the following Prayers (which He taught her) for a whole year. When the year is up, you will have honored each one of My Wounds."*

*These prayers are published under sanction of the Decree of November 18, 1986, published in the Acts Apostolicae Sedis, Vol. 58, No. 16 of December 29, 1966. **PRAYERS** approved by Pope Pius IX , The Fifteen Prayers of Saint Bridget of Sweden.*

Pope Benedict XV *expressed himself as follows on the Revelations of St. Bridget: "The approbation of such revelations implies nothing more than, after mature examination, it is permissible to publish them for the unit of the faithful. Though they don't merit the same credence as the truths of religion, one can, however, believe them out of human faith, conforming to the rules of prudence by which they are probable, and supported by sufficient motives that one might believe in them piously."*

The 14th of June 1303, at the moment Bridget was born, Benedict, the curate of Rasbo, prayed for the happy deliverance of Ingeborde. Suddenly he found himself enveloped by a luminous cloud out of which Our Lady appeared: "A child has been born at Birger; her voice will be heard by the entire world." Sagii, die XXIV Aprilis 1903

Pope Pius IX took cognizance of these Prayers with the prologue; he approved them May 31, 1862, recognizing them as true and for the good of souls.

THESE PRAYERS CAN SERVE AS THE WAY OF THE CROSS. Visitors to the Church of St. Paul at Rome can see the crucifix, above the Tabernacle in the Blessed Sacrament Chapel, sculptured by Pierre Cavallini, before which St. Bridget knelt when she received these 15 Prayers from Our Lord. The following inscription is placed in the church to commemorate the event: "Pendentis, Pendente Dei verba accepit aure accipit et verbum corde Brigitta Deum. Anno Jubilei MCCCL."

ST. BRIDGET PRAYERS HONORING THE WOUNDS OF CHRIST:

First Prayer
Our Father – Hail Mary.
O Jesus Christ! Eternal Sweetness to those who love Thee, joy surpassing all joy and all desire, Salvation and Hope of all sinners, Who hast proved that Thou hast no greater desire than to be among men, even assuming human nature at the fullness of time for the love of men, recall all the sufferings Thou hast endured from the instant of Thy conception, and especially during Thy Passion, as it was decreed and ordained from all eternity in the Divine plan. Remember, O Lord, that during the Last Supper with Thy disciples, having washed their feet, Thou gavest them Thy Most Precious Body and Blood, and while at the same time Thou didst sweetly console them, Thou didst foretell them Thy coming Passion. Remember the sadness and bitterness which Thou didst experience in Thy Soul as Thou Thyself bore witness saying: "My Soul is sorrowful even unto death." Remember all the fear, anguish and

pain that Thou didst suffer in Thy delicate Body before the torment of the Crucifixion, when, after having prayed three times, bathed in a sweat of blood, Thou wast betrayed by Judas, Thy disciple, arrested by the people of a nation Thou hadst chosen and elevated, accused by false witnesses, unjustly judged by three judges during the flower of Thy youth and during the solemn Paschal season. Remember that Thou wast despoiled of Thy garments and clothed in those of derision; that Thy Face and Eyes were veiled, that Thou wast buffeted, crowned with thorns, a reed placed in Thy Hands, that Thou was crushed with blows and overwhelmed with affronts and outrages. In memory of all these pains and sufferings which Thou didst endure before Thy Passion on the Cross, grant me before my death true contrition, a sincere and entire confession, worthy satisfaction and the remission of all my sins. Amen

Second Prayer
Our Father – Hail Mary.
O Jesus! True liberty of angels, Paradise of delights, remember the horror and sadness which Thou didst endure when Thy enemies, like furious lions, surrounded Thee, and by thousands of insults, spits, blows, lacerations and other unheard-of-cruelties, tormented Thee at will. In consideration of these torments and insulting words, I beseech Thee, O my Savior, to deliver me from all my enemies, visible and invisible, and to bring me, under Thy protection, to the perfection of eternal salvation. Amen

Third Prayer
Our Father – Hail Mary.
O Jesus! Creator of Heaven and earth Whom nothing can encompass or limit, Thou Who dost enfold and hold all under Thy Loving power, remember the very bitter pain Thou didst suffer when the Jews nailed Thy Sacred Hands and Feet to the Cross by blow after blow with big blunt nails, and not finding Thee in a pitiable enough state to satisfy their rage, they enlarged Thy Wounds, and added pain to pain, and with indescribable cruelty

stretched Thy Body on the Cross, pulled Thee from all sides, thus dislocating Thy Limbs. I beg of Thee, O Jesus, by the memory of this most Loving suffering of the Cross, to grant me the grace to fear Thee and to Love Thee. Amen.

Fourth Prayer
Our Father – Hail Mary.
O Jesus! Heavenly Physician, raised aloft on the Cross to heal our wounds with Thine, remember the bruises which Thou didst suffer and the weakness of all Thy Members which were distended to such a degree that never was there pain like unto Thine. From the crown of Thy Head to the Soles of Thy Feet there was not one spot on Thy Body that was not in torment, and yet , forgetting all Thy sufferings, Thou didst not cease to pray to Thy heavenly Father for Thy enemies, saying "Father forgive them for they know not what they do." Through this great Mercy, and in memory of this suffering, grant that the remembrance of Thy Most Bitter Passion may effect in us a perfect contrition and the remission of all our sins. Amen.

Fifth Prayer
Our Father – Hail Mary.
O Jesus! Mirror of eternal splendor, remember the sadness which Thou experienced, when contemplating in the light of Thy Divinity the predestination of those who would be saved by the merits of Thy Sacred passion, Thou didst see at the same time, the great multitude of reprobates who would be damned for their sins, and Thou didst complain bitterly of those hopeless lost and unfortunate sinners. Through this abyss of compassion and pity, and especially through the goodness which Thou displayed to the good thief when Thou sadist to him: "This day, thou shalt be with Me in paradise." I beg of Thee, O Sweet Jesus, that at the hour of my death, Thou wilt show me mercy. Amen.

Sixth Prayer
Our Father – Hail Mary.

O Jesus! Beloved and most desirable King, remember the grief Thou didst suffer, when naked and like a common criminal, Thou was fastened and raised on the Cross, when all Thy relatives and friends abandoned Thee, except Thy Beloved Mother, who remained close to Thee during Thy agony and whom Thou didst entrust to Thy faithful disciple when Thou sadist to Mary: "Woman, behold thy son!" and to St. John: "Son, behold thy Mother!" I beg of Thee O my Savior, by the sword of sorrow which pierced the soul of Thy holy Mother, to have compassion on me in all my affliction and tribulations, both corporal and spiritual, and to assist me in all my trials, and especially at the hour of my death. Amen

Seventh Prayer
Our Father – Hail Mary.

O Jesus! Inexhaustible Fountain of compassion, Who by a profound gesture of Love, said from the Cross: "I thirst!" suffered from the thirst for the salvation of the human race. I beg of Thee O my Savior, to inflame in our hearts the desire to tend toward perfection in all our acts; and to extinguish in us the concupiscence of the flesh and the ardor of worldly desires. Amen

Eighth Prayer
Our Father – Hail Mary.

O Jesus! Sweetness of hearts, delight of the spirit, by the bitterness of the vinegar and gall which Thou didst taste on the Cross for Love of us, grant us the grace to receive worthily Thy Precious Body and Blood during our life and at the hour of our death, that they may serve as a remedy and consolation for our souls. Amen

Ninth Prayer
Our Father – Hail Mary.
O Jesus! Royal virtue, joy of the mind, recall the pain Thou didst
endure when, plunged in an ocean of bitterness at the approach of
death, insulted, outraged by the Jews, Thou didst cry out in a loud
voice that Thou was abandoned by Thy Father, saying: "My God,
My God, why hast Thou forsaken me?" Through this anguish, I beg
of Thee, O my Savior, not to abandon me in the terrors and pains of
my death. Amen

Tenth Prayer
Our Father – Hail Mary.
O Jesus! Who art the beginning and end of all things, life and
virtue, remember that for our sakes Thou was plunged in an abyss of
suffering from the soles of Thy Feet to the crown of Thy Head. In
consideration of the enormity of Thy Wounds, teach me to keep,
through pure love, Thy Commandments, whose way is wide and
easy for those who love Thee. Amen

Eleventh Prayer
Our Father – Hail Mary.
O Jesus! Deep abyss of mercy, I beg of Thee, in memory of Thy
Wounds which penetrated to the very marrow of Thy Bones and to
the depth of Thy being, to draw me, a miserable sinner,
overwhelmed by my offenses, away from sin and to hide me from
Thy Face justly irritated against me, hide me in Thy Wounds, until
Thy anger and just indignation shall have passed away. Amen

Twelfth Prayer
Our Father – Hail Mary.
O Jesus! Mirror of Truth, symbol of unity, link of Charity, remember the multitude of wounds with which Thou was covered from head to foot, torn and reddened by the spilling of Thy adorable blood. O great and universal pain which Thou didst suffer in Thy virginal flesh for love of us! Sweetest Jesus!

What is there that Thou couldst have done for us which Thou hast not done! May the fruit of Thy sufferings be renewed in my soul by the faithful remembrance of Thy passion, and may Thy love increase in my heart each day, until I see Thee in eternity, Thou Who art the treasury of every real good and every joy, which I beg Thee to grant me, O sweetest Jesus, in Heaven. Amen

Thirteenth Prayer
Our Father – Hail Mary.
O Jesus! Strong Lion, Immortal and Invincible King, remember the pain which Thou didst endure when all Thy strength, both moral and physical, was entirely exhausted, Thou didst bow Thy head, saying: "It is consummated!" Through this anguish and grief, I beg of Thee Lord Jesus, to have mercy on me at the hour of my death when my mind will be greatly troubled and my soul will be in anguish. Amen

Fourteenth Prayer
Our Father – Hail Mary.
O Jesus! Only Son of the Father, splendor and figure of His substance remember the simple and humble recommendation Thou didst make of Thy Soul to Thy Eternal Father, saying: "Father, into Thy Hands I commend My Spirit!" And with Thy body all torn, and Thy Heart broken, and the bowels of Thy mercy open to redeem us, Thou didst expire.

By this precious death, I beg of Thee O King of Saints, comfort me and help me to resist the devil, the flesh and the world, so that being dead to the world I may live for Thee alone. I beg of Thee at the hour of my death to receive me, a pilgrim and an exile returning to Thee. Amen

Fifteenth Prayer
Our Father – Hail Mary.
O Jesus! True and fruitful Vine! Remember the abundant outpouring of Blood which Thou didst so generously shed from Thy Sacred Body as juice from grapes in a wine press. From Thy Side, pierced with a lance by a soldier, blood and water issued forth until there was not left in Thy Body a single drop, and finally, like a bundle of myrrh lifted to the top of the Cross, Thy delicate flesh was destroyed, the very Substance of Thy Body withered, and the Marrow of Thy Bones dried up. Through this bitter Passion and through the outpouring of Thy precious Blood, I beg of Thee, O Sweet Jesus, to receive my soul when I am in my death agony. Amen

Conclusion O Sweet Jesus! Pierce my heart so that my tears of penitence and love will be my bread day and night; may I be converted entirely to Thee, may my heart be Thy perpetual habitation, may my conversation be pleasing to Thee, and may the end of my life be so praiseworthy that I may merit Heaven and there with Thy saints, praise Thee forever. Amen.

Pope John Paul II on St Bridget of Sweden: His Holiness John Paul II began the Jubilee, on 1 October 1999, by proclaiming Saints Birgitta of Sweden, Catherine of Siena and Teresa Benedicta of the Cross (Edith Stein), Co-Patronesses of Europe.

Excerpts see full text: http://www.umilta.net/europe.html

POPE JOHN PAUL II APOSTOLIC LETTER ISSUED *MOTU PROPRIO*

PROCLAIMING SAINT BRIDGET OF SWEDEN, SAINT CATHERINE OF SIENA AND SAINT TERESA BENEDICTA OF THE CROSS CO-PATRONESSES OF EUROPE

"Even more than these devout pilgrimages, it was a profound sense of the mystery of Christ and the Church which led Bridget to take part in building up the ecclesial community at a quite critical period in the Church's history. Her profound union with Christ was accompanied by special gifts of revelation, which made her a point of reference for many people in the Church of her time. Bridget was recognized as having the power of prophecy, and at times her voice did seem to echo that of the great prophets of old. She spoke unabashedly to princes and pontiffs, declaring God's plan with regard to the events of history. She was not afraid to deliver stern admonitions about the moral reform of the Christian people and the clergy themselves (cf. *Revelations.*, IV, 49/1 ; cf. also IV, 5/2). Understandably, some aspects of her remarkable mystical output raised questions at the time; the Church's discernment constantly referred these back to public revelation alone, which has its fullness in Christ and its normative expression in Sacred Scripture. Even the experiences of the great Saints are not free of those limitations which always accompany the human reception of God's voice.

Yet there is no doubt that the Church, which recognized Bridget's holiness without ever pronouncing on her individual revelations, has accepted the overall authenticity of her interior experience. She stands as an important witness to the place reserved in the Church for a charism lived in complete docility to the Spirit of God and in full accord with the demands of ecclesial communion.

In a special way too, because the Scandinavian countries from which Bridget came were separated from full communion with the See of Rome during the tragic events of the sixteenth century, the figure of this Swedish Saint remains a precious ecumenical 'bridge', strengthened by the ecumenical commitment of her Order" -**Pope John Paul II**

SEVEN OBLATIONS OF THE MOST ADORABLE BLOOD OF OUR LORD JESUS CHRIST

Eternal Father, I offer Thee the merits of the most precious Blood of Jesus, Thy beloved Son, and my divine Redeemer, for the propagation and exaltation of our beloved and holy Mother, the Church; for the preservation and prosperity of her visible head, the Sovereign Pontiff and Bishop of Rome; for the Cardinals, Bishops, and Pastors of souls, and for all the Ministers of the sanctuary.

Then say Glory Be To The Father... and the following Aspiration: May benediction and thanks be always given to Jesus, Who has saved us by His Blood.

2. Eternal Father, I offer Thee the merits of the most precious Blood of Jesus, Thy beloved Son, and my divine Redeemer, for the peace and concord of Catholic kings and princes, for the humiliation of the enemies of our holy Faith, and for the happiness of the Christian people.

Glory Be To The Father, May benediction and thanks be always given to Jesus, Who has saved us by His Blood.

3. Eternal Father, I offer Thee the merits of the most precious Blood of Jesus, Thy beloved Son, and my divine Redeemer, for the enlightening of infidels, the extirpation of all heresies, and the conversion of sinners.

Glory Be To The Father, May benediction and thanks be always given to Jesus, Who has saved us by His Blood.

4. Eternal Father, I offer Thee the merits of the most precious Blood of Jesus, . Thy beloved Son, and my divine Redeemer, for all my relatives, friends, and enemies; for the poor, the sick, and the afflicted, and for all those for whom Thou knows and wills that I should pray.

Glory Be To The Father, May benediction and thanks be always given to Jesus, Who has saved us by His Blood.

5. Eternal Father, I offer Thee the merits of the most precious Blood of Jesus, Thy beloved Son, and my divine Redeemer, for those, who depart from this life today, that Thou may free them from the pains of hell, and may grant them a speedily admittance in the presence of Thy glory.

Glory Be To The Father, May benediction and thanks be always given to Jesus, Who has saved us by His Blood

6. Eternal Father, I offer Thee the merits of the most precious Blood of Jesus, Thy beloved Son, and my divine Redeemer, for all those who esteem this great treasure of His Sacred Blood, for those who are united with me in adoring and honoring it, and finally for those who endeavor to promote this holy devotion.

Glory Be To The Father, May benediction and thanks be always given to Jesus, Who has saved us by His Blood.

7. Eternal Father, I offer Thee the merits of the most precious Blood of Jesus, Thy beloved Son, and my divine Redeemer, for all my spiritual and temporal wants, for the relief of the holy souls in purgatory, and especially for those who have been most devoted to

the price of our Redemption, and to the dolours and sufferings of the Blessed Virgin Mary, our beloved Mother.

Glory Be To The Father, May benediction and thanks be always given to Jesus, Who has saved us by His Blood.

Glory be to the Sacred Blood of Jesus. Christ, now and at all times, and for all eternity. Amen.

INDULGENCES: 3 years for each recital. Plenary, once a month, on the usual conditions, for those who have recited them daily during the month. - Pen., 12 May 1931.

ST ANTHONY OF PADUA is one of my favorite saints. A tireless servant of God and miracle worker. St. Anthony started as an Augustine priest. He was humbled and greatly inspired when he witnessed the funeral precession of the remains of several Franciscans who were martyred in Morocco for preaching the Holy Gospel to Muslims. St. Anthony at that moment wanted to join the Franciscans and become a martyr. Well God had other plans for him. St. Anthony would become an incredible preacher and Doctor of the Church. Christ performed countless miracles through St. Anthony thus, the title 'Miracle worker'. He was the only saint in Catholic Church history to be canonized less than one year after his death. One of the many miracles that occurred was the appearance of the Christ Child with St. Anthony.

To learn more about this wonderful humble servant of Christ. visit: Http://www.capuchinfriars.org.au/saints/anthony.shtml

St. Anthony of Padua Novena

O wonderful St. Anthony, glorious on account of the fame of your miracles, and through the condescension of Jesus in coming in the form of a little child to rest in your arms, obtain for me of His bounty the grace which I ardently desire from the depths of my heart . (*State your intention*) You who were so compassionate toward miserable sinners, regard not the unworthiness of those who pray to you, but the glory of God that it may once again be magnified by the granting of the particular request (*State your intention*) which I now ask for with persevering earnestness. Amen

Pray one Our Father, one Hail Mary, and
Glory Be to the Father. Saint Anthony, pray for us!

DAY ONE

O holy St. Anthony, gentlest of saints, your love for God and charity for his creatures made you worthy while on earth to possess miraculous powers. Miracles waited your word, which you were ever ready to speak for those in trouble or anxiety. Encouraged by this thought, I implore you to obtain for me the favor I seek in this novena (*State your intention*). The answer to my prayer may require a miracle; even so, you are the saint of miracles. O gentle and loving Saint Anthony, whose heart was ever full of human sympathy, whisper my petition into the ears of the Infant Jesus, who loved to be folded in your arms, and the gratitude of my heart will always be yours.

SIC DEVS DILEXIT MVNDVM

One Our Father, one Hail Mary, and Glory Be to the Father. Saint Anthony, pray for us!

DAY TWO

O miracle-working St. Anthony, remember that it never has been heard that you left without help or relief anyone who in his need had recourse to you. Animated now with the most lively confidence, even with full conviction of not being refused, I fly for refuge to thee, O most favored friend of the Infant Jesus. O eloquent preacher of the divine mercy, despise not my supplications but, bringing them before the throne of God, strengthen them by your intercession and obtain for me the favor I seek in this novena (*State your intention*) .

One Our Father, one Hail Mary, and Glory Be to the Father. Saint Anthony, pray for us!

DAY THREE

O purest St. Anthony, who through your angelic virtue was made worthy to be caressed by the Divine Child Jesus, to hold him in your arms and press him to your heart. I entreat you to cast a benevolent glance upon me. O glorious St. Anthony, born under the protection of Mary Immaculate, on the Feast of her Assumption into Heaven, and consecrated to her and now so powerful an intercessor in Heaven, I beseech you to obtain for me the favor I ask in this novena (*State your intention*). O great wonder-worker, intercede for me that God may grant my request.

One Our Father, one Hail Mary, and Glory Be to the Father. Saint Anthony, pray for us!

DAY FOUR

I salute and honor you, O powerful helper, St. Anthony. The Christian world confidently turns to you and experiences your tender compassion and powerful assistance in so many necessities and sufferings that I am encouraged in my need to seek your help in obtaining a favorable answer to my request for the favor I seek in this novena (*State your intention*). O holy St. Anthony, I beseech you, obtain for me the grace that I desire.

One Our Father, one Hail Mary, and Glory Be to the Father. Saint Anthony, pray for us!

DAY FIVE

I salute you, St. Anthony, lily of purity, ornament and glory of Christianity. I salute you, great Saint, cherub of wisdom and seraph of divine love. I rejoice at the favors our Lord has so liberally bestowed upon you. In humility and confidence I entreat you to help me, for I know that God has given you charity and pity, as well as power. I ask you by the love you did feel toward the Infant Jesus as you held him in your arms to tell Him now of the favor I seek through your intercession in this novena (*State your intention*).

One Our Father, one Hail Mary, and Glory Be to the Father. Saint Anthony, pray for us!

DAY SIX

O glorious St. Anthony, chosen by God to preach his Word, you received from Him the gift of tongues and the power of working the most extraordinary miracles. O good St. Anthony, pray that I may fulfill the will of God in all things so that I may love Him, with you, for all eternity. O kind St. Anthony, I beseech you, obtain for me the grace that I desire, the favor I seek in this novena (*State your intention*).

SIC DEVS DILEXIT MVNDVM

One Our Father, one Hail Mary, and Glory Be to the Father. Saint Anthony, pray for us!

DAY SEVEN

O renowned champion of the faith of Christ, most holy St. Anthony, glorious for your many miracles, obtain for me from the bounty of my Lord and God the grace which I ardently seek in this novena (*State your intention*) . O holy St. Anthony, ever attentive to those who invoke you, grant me that aid of your powerful intercession.

One Our Father, one Hail Mary, and Glory Be to the Father. Saint Anthony, pray for us!

DAY EIGHT

O holy St. Anthony, you have shown yourself so powerful in your intercession, so tender and so compassionate towards those who honor you and invoke you in suffering and distress. I beseech you most humbly and earnestly to take me under your protection in my present necessities and to obtain for me the favor I desire (*State your intention*). Recommend my request to the merciful Queen of Heaven, that she may plead my cause with you before the throne of her Divine Son.

One Our Father, one Hail Mary, and Glory Be to the Father. Saint Anthony, pray for us!

DAY NINE

Saint Anthony, servant of Mary, glory of the Church, pray for our Holy Father, our bishops, our priests, our Religious Orders, that, through their pious zeal and apostolic labors, all may be united in faith and give greater glory to God. St. Anthony, helper of all who invoke you, pray for me and intercede for me before the throne of Almighty God that I be granted the favor I so earnestly seek in this novena (*State your intention*).

SIC DEVS DILEXIT MVNDVM

One Our Father, one Hail Mary, and Glory Be to the Father. Saint Anthony, pray for us!
May the divine assistance remain always with us. Amen
May the souls of the faithful departed, through the mercy of God, rest in peace. Amen.

O God, may the votive commemoration of blessed Anthony, your confessor, be a source of joy to your Church, that she may always be fortified with spiritual assistance, and deserve to enjoy eternal rewards. Through Christ our Lord. Amen.

WHAT IS THE HOLY ROSARY

"After the Divine Office and the Holy Mass, no homage is as agreeable to Jesus and His Divine Mother as the fervent prayer of the Holy Rosary, since the work of salvation began with the Angelic Salutation (Hail Mary) the Salvation of each one of us in particular is attached to this prayer."

St. Dominic

Photograph taken by MSG Michael M. Cutone

"The Holy Rosary is not just a conglomeration of our Fathers and Hail Mary's, But on the contrary it is a Divine Summary of the Mysteries of the Life, Passion, Death, and Glory of Jesus and Mary."
St. Louis De Montfort

"The Rosary illuminates the mysteries of the Holy Gospel. It deepens our understanding and intimacy with Christ, and with the salvation history of the Gospel. This is why the Rosary is such a powerful prayer. Simply said, the Rosary is a prayer of the Gospel! While praying the Rosary, you are learning, and growing intimately with the Holy Gospel. After announcing each Mystery *(key events like the Birth of Christ, Agony in Garden, the Scourging at the pillar etc.)* you will recite one "Our Father" then ten "Hail Marys, and one "Glory Be." While reciting the Hail Marys, you are contemplating and reflecting on that particular significant event *(called a mystery)* of Christ and salvation history." *† MSG Michael Cutone*

> "The Blessed Mother herself refers to this battle of souls as warfare, and refers to the Rosary as a weapon. *"Dear Dominic, do you know which weapon the Blessed Trinity wants to use to reform the world?"*
> **St. Louis De Montfort** .The Secret of The Rosary..

"The Rosary comes from Latin and means a *crown of roses or garland of roses*; the saints have referred to it as a spiritual bouquet given to the Blessed Mother. The Rosary is the prayer of saints. The sheer numbers of saints (as well as several Doctors of The Church) who have sung the unending praises of the Rosary during their lives is compelling, and speaks volumes of the simplicity, depth, and beauty of this Gospel prayer.

As you pray the Rosary, your intimacy with the Gospel grows. Key salvation events in the life of Christ guide your prayers, thoughts, and actions. The Rosary is a beautiful prayer of the Gospel. The practice of the Rosary began around 1200 AD, probably as a combination of St. Dominic preaching the Rosary, and a practice that evolved by illiterate laity to imitate the monastic Divine Office (Breviary or Liturgy of the Hours); the laity would substitute 50, or even 150, Ave Marias (Hail Marys) for the Breviary's Psalms. The tradition of the Catholic Church teaches us the Blessed Mother presented the Rosary to St. Dominic to combat the Albigensian heresy, and sin. St. Dominic, armed with the Rosary (and his preaching skill) was incredibly effective with combating the

Albigensian heresy, and converting sinners. There is no question that St. Dominic and Blessed Alan de Roche played significant roles with spreading devotion to the Rosary." † *MSG Michael Cutone*

"The rosary is the book of the blind, where souls see and there enact the greatest drama of love the world has ever known; it is the book of the simple, which initiates them into mysteries and knowledge more satisfying than the education of other men; it is the book of the aged, whose eyes close upon the shadow of this world, and open on the substance of the next. The power of the rosary is beyond description." **Archbishop Fulton Sheen**

The rosary is made up of two things: mental prayer and vocal prayer. In the Holy Rosary mental prayer is none other than meditation of the chief mysteries of the life, death and glory of Jesus Christ and of His Blessed Mother. Vocal prayer consists in saying fifteen decades of the Hail Mary, each decade headed by an Our Father, while at the same time meditating on and contemplating the fifteen principal virtues which Jesus and Mary practiced in the fifteen mysteries of the Holy Rosary. In the first five decades we must honor the five Joyous Mysteries and meditate on them; in the second five decades the Sorrowful Mysteries and in the third group of five, the Glorious Mysteries. So the Rosary is a blessed blending of mental and vocal prayer by which we honor and learn to imitate the mysteries and virtues of the life, death, passion and glory of Jesus and Mary."
St. Louis De Montfort, The Secret of the Rosary.

REGARDING ST. LOUIS DE MONTFORT'S BOOK THE SECRET OF THE ROSARY.

Every Catholic and every Christian who reads this wonderful work by St. De Montfort would gain tremendous insight and depth of understanding with this Gospel prayer and the intercessory role of The Blessed Mother. The Secret of the Rosary. is an exhaustive work on the Rosary prayer; St. De Montfort accomplished a masterful job of unfolding the power, beautiful and truth regarding this Gospel prayer. I have read my copy numerous times, many pages are dogged ear, text highlighted or under lined. Each time I re-read this incredible book another truth is learned or "discovered" about the Gospel and The Rosary. Every Catholic and Christian should own a copy of this remarkable book a true blessing!

† MSG Michael Cutone

Canon Willam states; *"It goes far beyond mere research; we might say that it contains everything that can be said about the Rosary."*

ORIGIN OF THE ROSARY BY ST. LOUIS DE MONTFORT

"Since the Holy Rosary is composed, principally and in substance, of the Prayer of Christ and the Angelic Salutation, that is, the Our Father and the Hail Mary, it was without doubt the first prayer and the first devotion of the faithful and has been in use all through the centuries from the time of the Apostles and disciples down to the present. But it was only in the year 1214, however, that Holy Mother Church received the Rosary in its present form and according to the method we use today. It was given to the Church by Saint Dominic who had received it from the Blessed Virgin as a powerful means of converting the Albigensians and other sinners. I will tell you the story of how he received it, which is found in the very well-known book "De Dignitate Psalterii" by Blessed Alan de la Roche [1]. Saint Dominic, seeing that the gravity of people's sins was hindering the conversion of the Albigensians, withdrew into a forest near Toulouse where he prayed unceasingly for three days and three nights.

During this time he did nothing but weep and do harsh penances in order to appease the anger of Almighty God. He used his discipline so much that his body was lacerated, and finally he fell into a coma. At this point Our Lady appeared to him, accompanied by three angels, and she said: "Dear Dominic, do you know which weapon the Blessed Trinity wants to use to reform the world?"

"Oh, my Lady," answered Saint Dominic, "you know far better than I do because next to your Son Jesus Christ you have always been the chief instrument of our salvation." **St. Louis De Montfort** <u>The Secret of The Rosary</u>

St. Dominic presented with Holy Rosary from Blessed Mother

Then Our Lady replied: "I want you to know that, in this kind of warfare, the battering ram has always been the Angelic Psalter which is the foundation stone of the New Testament. Therefore if you want to reach these hardened souls and win them over to God, preach my Psalter." So he arose, comforted, and burning with zeal, for the conversion of the people in that district, he made straight for the Cathedral.

At once unseen angels rang the bells to gather the people together and Saint Dominic began to preach. At the very beginning of his sermon an appalling storm broke, out, the earth shook, the sun was darkened, and there was so much thunder and lightning that all were very much afraid."

Even greater was their fear when looking at a picture of Our Lady exposed in a prominent place they saw her raise her arms to heaven three times to call down God's vengeance upon them if they failed to be converted, to amend their lives, and seek the protection of the Holy Mother of God. God wished, by means of these supernatural phenomena, to spread the new devotion of the Holy Rosary and to make it more widely known.

At last, at the prayer of Saint Dominic, the storm came to an end, and he went on preaching. So fervently and compellingly did he explain the importance and value of the Holy Rosary that almost all the people of Toulouse embraced it and renounced their false beliefs. In a very short time a great improvement was seen in the town; people began leading Christian lives and gave up their former bad habits. [1]. De Dignitate Psalterii. The importance and Beauty of the Holy Rosary, by Blessed Alan de la Roche, O.P., French Dominican Father and Apostle of the Holy Rosary. "

>   **St. Louis De Montfort**, The Secret of the Rosary.

WHAT THE CHURCH SAINTS HAVE SAID ABOUT THE ROSARY

"'Hail Mary, full of grace, the Lord is with thee!' No creature has ever said anything that was more pleasing to me, nor will anyone ever be able to find or say to me anything that pleases me more."
Our Lady to St. Mechtilde

"If you say the Rosary faithfully until death, I assure you that in spite of the gravity of your sins, you shall receive a never-fading crown of glory. Even if you are on the brink of damnation, even if you have one foot in Hell, even if you have sold your soul to the devil as sorcerers do who practice black magic, and even if you are a heretic as obstinate as a devil, sooner or later you will be converted and will amend your life and save your soul, if and mark well what I say -- if you say the Holy Rosary devoutly every day until death for the purpose of knowing the truth and obtaining contrition and pardon of your sins." **St. Louis de Montfort**

"The Rosary is THE weapon." **St. Padre Pio** *(Stigmatic* Capuchin *Priest)*

"After the Divine Office and the Holy Mass, no homage is as agreeable to Jesus and His Divine Mother as the fervent prayer of the Holy Rosary, since the work of salvation began with the Angelic Salutation (Hail Mary) the Salvation of each one of us in particular is attached to this prayer." **St. Dominic**

"Among the devotion approved by the Church none have been so favored by so many miracles as the Holy Rosary."
Pope Pius IX

"The Hail Mary puts the devil to flight and causes Hell to Tremble with terror." **St. Bernard**

"When you say your Rosary the Angels rejoice, the Blessed Trinity delights in it, my Son finds joy in it too, and I myself am happier than you can possibly imagine. After the Holy Sacrifice of the Mass, there is nothing in the Church that I love as much as the Holy Rosary." **Our Lady to Blessed Alan**

"There is no surer means of calling down God's blessing upon the family.. than the daily recitation of the Rosary". **Pope Pius XII**

"The best method of prayer is the Holy Rosary if you Say it well."
St Francis de Sales (Doctor of the Church)

"I would Gladly suffer . . . Just to have the chance to pray even one Hail Mary in order to gain more merits before our lord."
St Teresa of Avila (Doctor of the Church)

"No one can live continually in sin and continue to say the Rosary-either he will give up sin or he will give up the Rosary."
Bishop Hugh Boyle

SIC DEVS DILEXIT MVNDVM

". . . Therefore we are sure that Our Children and all their brethren throughout the world will turn (the Rosary) into a school for learning true perfection, as, with a deep spirit of recollection, they contemplate the teachings that shine forth from the life of Christ and of Mary Most Holy." **Pope Paul XXIII**

"The Rosary is my favorite prayer. A marvelous prayer! Marvelous in its simplicity and in its depth. . .the simple prayer of the Rosary beats the rhythm of human life."
Pope John Paul II

THE HOLY ROSARY

"Praying the Holy Rosary is the equivalent to calling an air strike on Satan's position. The Rosary is without question the best weapon I ever carried or placed into operation against the enemy while on the field of battle."

† MSG Michael Cutone

1. Make the **Sign of the Cross** and say the Apostles Creed

Photograph taken by MSG Michael M. Cutone

2. On First large bead pray the Our Father

3. The three small beads pray three Hail Marys

4. Between small bead and large bead pray the Glory be to the Father…

5. Announce the First Mystery; then pray the Our Father

6. Pray ten Hail Marys, *(one decade)* while meditating on the Mystery *(The Specific Gospel Event)*

7. After the tenth Hail Mail pray the Glory be to the Father… Then Fatima Prayer

8. On large bead announce the Second Mystery; then pray the Our Father.

Repeat **6** and **7** and continue with Third, Fourth and Fifth Mysteries. Once all five decades are read, finish with Hail Holy Queen prayer. Remember we are asking for Mary's intercessions, to join us in prayer, to take our prayers to Christ. Bear in mind the profound love Jesus has for His mother and Mary's love for her Son. When Mary brings our prayers to her Son, how could we have a better advocate? The Mother of Jesus standing next to us when we approach God almighty. Sign me up!

HAIL, HOLY QUEEN, Mother of Mercy, our life, our sweetness and our hope! To thee do we cry, poor banished children of Eve; to thee do we send up our sighs, mourning and weeping in this valley of tears. Turn then, most gracious advocate, thine eyes of mercy toward us, and after this our exile, show unto us the blessed fruit of thy womb, Jesus. O clement, O loving, O sweet Virgin Mary!

V. Pray for us, O Holy Mother of God.
R. That we may be made worthy of the promises of Christ.

Let us pray. O GOD, whose only begotten Son, by His life, death, and resurrection, has purchased for us the rewards of eternal life, grant, we beseech Thee, that meditating upon these mysteries of the Most Holy Rosary of the Blessed Virgin Mary, we may imitate what they contain and obtain what they promise, through the same Christ Our Lord. Amen.

Joyful Mysteries
Monday and Saturday

The Annunciation	Luke 1:26-31
The Visitation	Luke 1:39-45
The Birth of Jesus	Luke 2:6-7
Presentation of Jesus at the Temple	Luke 2:29-32
The Finding of Jesus	Luke 2:49-50

Luminous Mysteries
Thursday

Baptism of Jesus in the Jordan River	Mark 1:9-11
The Wedding at Cana	John 2:1-12
Proclamation of the Kingdom	Mark 1:14-15
Transfiguration of Jesus	Mark 9:2-7
The Institution of the Eucharist	Luke 22:14-20

The Sorrowful Mysteries
Tuesday and Friday

Our Lord's Agony in the Garden	Luke 22:40-46
The Scourging at the Pillar	Mark 15:8-15
The Crowning with Thorns	Mark 15:16-20 / Isaiah 53:2-3
Jesus Carries the Cross	Luke 23:26-28 / 1 Peter 2:20-21
The Crucifixion	Luke 23:34/ Luke 23:44-47 / Psalm 22:2-5

The Glorious Mysteries
Sunday and Wednesday

The Resurrection of Jesus	Matthew 1:1-7
The Ascension	Luke 24:50-51
Descent of the Holy Spirit	Acts 2:1-4 / Romans 8:15
The Assumption of Mary	Judith 13:20
The Coronation of Mary	Luke 1:46-49

WORK CITED

Catechism of the Catholic Church. Libreria Editrice Vaticana 1997

St. Joseph Edition New American Bible. Catholic Book Publishing Corp., NJ 1992

The Post –Synodal Apostolic Exhortation of John Paul II **Pastores Dabo Vobis.** Libreria Editrice Vaticana 1992

St. Louis De Montfort. **The Secret Of The Rosary.** TAN Books and Publishers, Inc. IL Rockford 2000

St. Louis De Montfort. **True Devotion To Mary**. TAN Books and Publishers, Inc. IL Rockford 2000

Fr. Paul O' Sullivan. **The Wonders of the Mass.** Written in 1963 by Fr. Paul O'Sullivan, O.P., TAN Books and Publishers, Inc. IL Rockford 2000

Fr. Christopher Rengers, O.F.M. **The 33 Doctors Of The Church.** TAN Books and Publishers, Inc. IL Rockford 2000

Luigi Gambero, S.M., **Mary and the Fathers of the Church,** Ignatius press, 1999.

Cannon Francis Ripley. **This is The Faith.** TAN Books and Publishers, Inc. IL Rockford 2002

John C. Maxwell. **The Maxwell Leadership Bible.** Thomas Nelson, TN Nashville, 2003

The Dwight D. Eisenhower Presidential Library and Museum Website http://www.eisenhower.archives.gov/Research/Digital_Documents/Holocaust/1945_04_19_DDE_to_Marshall.pdf

Christopher Hollis, **The Jesuits: A History**. New York: Macmillan Company, 1968

Catholic Encyclopedia. Http://www.newadvent.org/cathen/06233b.htm